Dearest Annie,

You Wanted a Report on Berkson's Class:
Letters from Frances LeFevre to Anne Waldman

Frances LeFevre, 1944

Dearest Annie,

You Wanted a Report on Berkson's Class:
Letters from Frances LeFevre to Anne Waldman

Edited by Lisa Birman
Introduction by Bill Berkson
Afterword by Anne Waldman

Hanging Loose Press
Brooklyn, New York

Published by Hanging Loose Press, 231 Wyckoff Street, Brooklyn,
New York 11217-2208. All rights reserved. No part of this book may
be reproduced without the publisher's written permission, except for
brief quotations in reviews.

www.hangingloosepress.com

Printed in the United States of America
10 9 8 7 6 5 4 3 2 1

Hanging Loose Press thanks the Literature Program of the New York
State Council on the Arts for a grant in support of the publication of
this book.

Cover design: Marie Carter

Cover art: "Poem/Poem" collaboration by Joe Brainard and Anne
Waldman, collage, ink, pencil, 1978. Collection: Anne Waldman

ISBN 978-1-934909-90-4

Library of Congress cataologing-in-publication available on request.

Contents

Editor's Note

I came to the work of Frances LeFevre through her daughter, Anne Waldman. We worked together at Naropa University's Jack Kerouac School of Disembodied Poetics for twelve years, planning the Summer Writing Program and doing our best to "keep the world safe for poetry."

I was visiting Anne one afternoon when she pulled out a box of letters she'd just received from her archive at the University of Michigan. She had requested copies of correspondence with her mother. It was a treasure trove. The letters date from 1961 through 1981. Some years, when Anne was traveling or living out of New York, are thick with correspondence. Others, when they were both closer to home, are more sparse.

Frances was an icon of the New York poetry scene. An early marriage and travels to Greece instilled a lifelong love of Greek culture and literature, which informed her opinions on American happenings. Her endless curiosity saw her moving between art galleries, dance and music performances, poets theatre, lectures, and other cultural events. She combed bookstores for new voices and *samizdat* publications. She read everything. Through these letters, I felt myself transported to Greenwich Village in the 1960s.

"Form is never more than an extension of content," Robert Creeley told Charles Olson. Personal letters are a form for our most intimate content. They bridge the geographical divide between a writer and reader who find themselves in separate places or times. They hold memories, transmit daily details, secret confessions. A letter can be anything the writer declares. Perhaps that is true for any literary form. Frances would likely disagree. She had some clear ideas about various literary forms. But her letters make room for everything.

Of course, these are a mother's letters to her daughter. Through these letters we learn of Frances's aspirations for Anne. How she sees her capable of anything and everything, her insistence on greatness. Anne is never to court the ordinary. Not on Frances's watch.

As Anne and I looked through the box of letters, she filled me in on the who's who of their world. We immediately talked about publishing an excerpt. Anne hadn't re-read all the letters, many of them were close to fifty years old, but she handed me the box. I was struck by her willingness to reveal her familial lineage, to let her mother speak. Though these letters are from Frances to Anne, I have come to see the collection as a love letter from Anne to Frances.

As I worked my way through the letters, there was something so recognizable in Frances's communication. Here was the genesis of Anne's underlined words, her exclamation marks, her confidence of tone. Here, too, was the DNA that fostered her love for poetry and her endless energy. Through these letters we can trace Frances's lineage as a writer, how it branches and blooms into Anne's lineage.

Frances seemed to be in the midst of everything all the time. She was the epitome of a New York culture maven and of old bohemia. Her life was a constant flux of theatre, books, happenings, and philosophy. She had a lot of opinions, and Anne was her sounding board and confidante.

While the letters were composed on a variety of typewriters, and some were handwritten, there are remarkably few misspellings and typos. Frances was a stickler for correct grammar. She believed in rigor. If you're going to use a word, make sure it's the right word, make sure it's the best word, and make sure that you really mean it. She would occasionally scratch something out and correct it; every now and again she would take Anne to task for an "unforgiveable" grammatical mistake in a previous letter. She did guess at a few names, and those have been corrected whenever errors were identified. The one exception is Peter Schjeldahl's name, which must have puzzled many, and which Frances herself noted with excitement when she finally settled on the correct spelling. While most of the letters are dated, some are not. We did our best to place them in the correct order. A few passages were also edited for content and context.

In addition to the letters, Anne kept various poems that Frances sent to her over the years. Unfortunately, not all of the poems referenced in the letters were found. Relevant clippings that Frances enclosed with her letters had also disappeared from their envelopes.

Scattered throughout the letters are treatises on art, on poetry, on family, on feminism. In reading the larger collection, I gravitated towards poetry, as Frances often did. Frances took two classes at the New School with Bill Berkson. The first, in 1966, came during Anne's final semester at Bennington College. Anne had asked Frances to keep her posted on the workshop, and Frances took copious notes, creating a kind of correspondence course in which she related their readings, discussions, and writing exercises. Her classmates included some of New York's most important up and coming writers—Hannah Weiner, Bernadette Mayer, Michael Brownstein, and Peter Schjeldahl, amongst others.

Thirty-three years after this incredible confluence of poetic energy, I had my own experience as a student in Bill Berkson's workshop, this time at Naropa University. I remember his class as equal parts community and commitment. I was diving into a study of New York School collaboration, and found myself gazing back at what was such a generative time. He reminded me to also set my gaze ahead. To find community amongst my peers as well as in my lineage.

Through Bill Berkson's workshop, Frances and I became classmates. Though she was no longer alive when I took Bill's class, we shared the experience of his experience. It quickly became clear that Frances's record of Bill's class was the first treasure to be mined. There are many more. Throughout the years, Frances continued to write about poetry—her own work, her championing of Anne's writing, her translations of Angelos Sikelianos's writing, her stint as editor of the Poetry Project Newsletter, her opinions about whose writing had it and who was a big fuss about nothing.

Fifteen years after our workshop, I remain grateful to Bill Berkson for his teachings about poetry and about being a poet. As I am to Frances and to Anne, from whom I have learned so much both in and out of these letters.

—Lisa Birman, 2015

With Frances (& Others) at the New School

I had been living in Paris for about six months when, in either January or February, 1964, Frank O'Hara wrote to say that Kenneth Koch, who had been my teacher only five years earlier, wanted to recommend me to teach a poetry workshop at the New School starting that coming summer, and if I was interested I should get a proposal to him, Kenneth, immediately. It worked, and summer 1964 I began my five-year tenure at the New School. Somehow I believed that I had been meant to replace Kenneth, who by then was fully occupied with his professorial duties at Columbia, but now I find that he continued at the New School off and on for a couple more years.

Course Description

1672 Poetry: reading and writing

Tuesdays 8:10-9:30 P.M., beginning February 1. $60. (Reg. fee: p. 6).

William C. Berkson

For those who have had some experience in writing poetry. Students' poems are read and discussed in class and seen in relation to issues raised by a few well-known poems read closely during the term. The purpose is to increase awareness of the possibilities and problem involved in writing contemporary poetry. Some of the poems read are: Williams' Asphodel, *Pound's* Cantos, *Wyatt's sonnets, Joyce's* Finnegans Wake. *Some of the issues: The Personality of the Poet, Speech and Typing, Poetry as Narration, Poetry as Ethics, Group Composition. Guest poets join in certain discussions.*

—The New School
Bulletin, Spring 1966

The reading list changed over the years, as did I. Williams, Rimbaud, O'Hara, Wieners, Auden, Keats, Pope, Ashbery, Stein, Ginsberg, Blake and Lorca put in appearances, but the basic format of the class stayed pretty much the same. Despite the fact that I had already published a lot of poetry under the name "Bill Berkson," it was difficult in those days for institutions to accept "Bill" instead of "William" (or "William C.") in catalogue listings, bylines or on mastheads. (At *ARTnews*, where I worked in the early 60s, I was always "William", or, in the Reviews and Previews section, "W.B."; in other art publications, the same rule applied well into the 1970s.) Regardless of nomenclature, in the process of those initial years as a teacher, I went from being a protegé of the older generation of New York poets to encountering poets my own age—from the odd angle of posing as their teacher—and eventually finding something of my own place among them.

The New School in those years was bubbling. For Spring 1959, the semester that I took Kenneth Koch's workshop, the bulletin listed John Cage's courses in Experimental Composition and Mushroom Identification (the latter categorized under "Recreation"), Rollo May on "Zen and Existentialism," and other offerings taught by Erich Fromm, William Troy, Alfred Kazin, and Louise Varese. Frank O'Hara taught a workshop there in spring 1963. By 1966, the writing faculty included, beside Kenneth and me, LeRoi Jones, Arnold Weinstein, Jose Garcia Villa, Marguerite Young, Robert Phelps, Diane Wakoski, David Ignatow, and Michael Rumaker. Henry Cowell and Martin Williams taught music, Joseph Chaikin theater, and William K. Everson a course on film. September–November, 1966, featured a series of "Readings by young poets in the vanguard tradition," with Ted Berrigan, Ed Sanders, Ron Padgett, Dick Gallup, Aram Saroyan, David Antin, Joseph Ceravolo, Jim Brodey and others. That last list is telling: none of the poets who read in what must have been a remarkably exciting series showed up in my classes—Ted Berrigan had his own workshop across town at the Poetry Project—but they were part of the buzz I was then becoming privy to. The New School credit rolls for my workshop in the fall 1965 and spring 1966 semesters included (names here as registered) Michael Brownstein, Bernadette F. Mayer, and Peter C.

Schjeldahl. Through the years, such notables as Lee Crabtree, Hannah Weiner, Rebecca Wright, Charles North, Musa McKim, Joachim Neugroschel, Carter Ratcliff, Mary Ferrari, John Godfrey, and Jim Carroll came and went. Among the early contingent, Peter Schjeldahl, for one, was taking both Ted Berrigan's and my classes, and Bernadette may well have followed suit.

In 1966 Frances was 55, a fairly average age for those attending writing classes at the New School in those days. There was a noticeable divide socially between the older students, most of whom were women, and the young ones, who tended to be more evenly mixed in gender and generally more ambitious about being writers. Probably the closest in Frances' circle of workshop friends was Jean Boudin, whose husband Leonard was a prominent civil rights lawyer; their daughter, Kathy, was one of the Weathermen responsible for, among other things, the premature detonation of a bomb that wrecked a house on East 11th Street in 1970. Others whom Frances befriended in the class were Mary Ferrari and Miriam Solan. Later, she also became close with Patti Smith who appeared—first name "Hatti" then—in the workshop for a semester, in the late '60s.

You wanted a report on Berkson's class.

—Frances LeFevre to Anne Waldman,
[undated, mid-March], 1966.

That Anne would have asked Frances to send her these reports, after having accompanied her mother one evening early on that spring, is flattering. By this time, in her final semester at Bennington, Anne was already a poet, possessed of her own mind, taste and inclination, and on the verge of entering like the proverbial ball of fire the atmosphere of contemporary New York poetry. The previous year, inspired by what she heard at the Berkeley Poetry Conference, she had affirmed her commitment to her chosen art by way of a formal vow. In retrospect, Anne's commitment appears to have been a firmer one than I myself had made by then. No matter how serious and assured I may have seemed in class, my own work at the time, not to mention my personal life, was in the doldrums, for which my authoritative classroom manner, signaled by the rather haughty course description quoted above, was a partial coverup.

He had a large pile of poems to hand back to the class—he said they were all that had been handed in to date—but had time to read only two which he said came off—my IRENE and one by the dark girl. . . .

Our next assignment is to write a poem with each verse in a different form, with at least three verses of which the middle one (if 3) is to be a limerick.

—Frances LeFevre to Anne Waldman,
[undated, mid-March], 1966.

An impossible assignment—what was I thinking? But Frances was right on it; in fact, she may have been the only one to actually fulfill it: "Last Tuesday I turned in my 3-part assignment, consisting of 4 short couplets, one limerick, and ten lines in *terza rima* . . . " In her letters, the workshop is "Berkson's class," and I am "Berkson" or "BB" while the addressee—Frances's daughter Anne, who turned 21 in the middle of that semester—is "Annie." There were plenty of people who sat in those New School classes simply to pass the time—to soak up a little culture, as it were, or just to try out various forms of self-expression— but Frances wasn't one of them. The letters show how serious she was about every aspect of the class, and about poetry in general. In them, you can find her pondering, sometimes deeply puzzling over, what may have seemed to me the slightest remark of that week's session. Her hearing of whatever I said is very much hers, and often a conundrum to me, in turn. (Was I really so untoward as to discourage Hannah Weiner from using colors in her poems?)

As the weeks, and their concomitant letters, progress, she takes careful note, as well, of my wardrobe changes for class ("He is such a dandy"), and speculates, given amply conflicting shards of evidence, about my sexual preferences. She considers every writing assignment

14

and how it fits with what she has already been up to. The assigned readings—especially O'Hara, Ashbery, Ginsberg—create minor crises, soon overcome, in her principles and taste. (About O'Hara: "He didn't bewilder me but I read hastily and didn't see the depths.") With a dramatist's eye, she watches personal relations among the younger students unfold and, in her reports to Anne, comments upon them and also tells how she sees the more senior ones, often saltily but sometimes with great empathy. We read more of "the dark girl" (Bernadette again), who "never opens her mouth in class . . . probably an introvert"; the "obnoxious" old man Frances "can't help pitying because he is so not with it and yet he keeps trying"; and then how, in an extracurricular perception, Jean Boudin "seems to operate on intuition rather than rational thought."

Frances's own demeanor, or how I picture it now, was at once commanding and, for me anyway, hard to read. Her dominant shade was a sort of chestnut brown, with highlights. Her well-practiced skepticism manifested itself with a perpetual smirk. Yet she was bright-eyed, kind, observant and endlessly curious, and those qualities eventually made her an integral part of the downtown world of younger poets that her daughter did so much to bring together. If Frances was seen attending a reading at the Poetry Project or an opening at some new artists' space, you knew it was an event of some significance. As Anne says later in this book, "She had a charged almost aspirational energy, to *know* and to understand what made people tick; to know more about poetry, about how *that* worked . . ."

—Bill Berkson, 2015

The Letters

[undated, probably mid–March 1966]
Wednesday morning

Dearest Annie,

You wanted a report on Berkson's class. Last night's was very good, even better than the one you attended. B. started out by saying people are turning in so many poems on "social subjects"—civil rights, the Viet Nam war, etc. (you can imagine them all, as I can) and he was going to try to show how they should not be done because they are practically all wrong. Said people make a statement of some violent emotion and then put what he called a series of "notations", meaning images that have some associative meaning to themselves on the subject but to nobody else and rarely suggest anything to him. He suggested that they try to express their thoughts in simple complete declarative sentences for a while with strict attention to English grammar and maybe eventually they'll find out how to think clearly and make clear statements. Quote from him:

"The only reason for a lack of clear statement in any writing is either you feel your thought is too complex to be stated in clear short sentences (and most thoughts are not) or you are sitting in a different realm of language where your aim is not just simple expository statement."

I suppose the latter realm is where Ashbery sits. B. read several examples of poems which express feelings about outside (not necessarily political or social, but personal too) situations indirectly and successfully: Auden's IN MEMORY OF W.B.YEATS, Pound's translation EXILE'S LETTER, parts of Williams' THE DESCENT and ASPHODEL THAT GREENY FLOWER and several shorter things of his, one by MacNeice (Interesting type!) title forgotten, and Pound's section IV from HUGH SELWYN MAUBERLEY beginning "These fought in any case / and some believing", which he said is a more effective anti-war poem than anything being written about Viet Nam. He read with a lot of feeling, quite beautifully.

He's against using too many participial forms unless they are indispensable for expressing a specific meaning. He is also against empty spaces and dots and dropping punctuation unless ditto—said bad poets use all these devices sloppily and they are mostly ridiculous and we ought all to go straight back to first-grade grammar and sentence construction.

He also said he couldn't care less whether a writer is angry, passionate, indignant, sensitive, or whatnot. The test is the composition itself and how it stands up alone and that's where the ruthlessness of poetry comes in. If we find careful composition tedious that's just too bad.

He had a large pile of poems to hand back to the class—he said they were all that have been handed in to date—but had time to read only two which he said came off—my IRENE and one by the dark girl who comes to class with Peter Scheldahjl. Her name is Miss Mayer and that's why I confused her name with that of the other girl (Myers) and obviously she is the one P.S. had mentioned to you as being good. Her poem was short but very nice—Ashbery-ish, conveying its own integral sense of logic and suggestions. She looked very happy at being praised.

That old man in the class was sort of obnoxious. I can't help pitying him because he is so not with it and yet he keeps trying. He stated that he had taken the class mainly in order to find out why he likes certain poems and not others (in itself that's nothing wrong) but he still thinks rhymed poetry is better poetry. B. tries to be patient with him but what can he say? Then at the end when B. was handing back poems and calling out people's names the old man kept interjecting "Ashbery!", "Ginsberg!" Everybody just ignored him.

BB evidently made it up to WRVR because he told me he had got SILO [Bennington College literary magazine, AW was the editor] and liked it. I showed him the MACARONIC POETRY and he got very enthusiastic and asked to borrow it and promised to give it back so I had to let him take it. He even read one of the centos to the class.

Our next assignment is to write a poem with each verse in a different form, with at least three verses of which the middle one (if 3) is to be a limerick. I finally managed to produce one on Monday in time to turn in and enclose (started to make copy but decided to change some of it so will send it later) it since you want to see what I'm doing, although I intend to work over it some more after I see what he says.

Yesterday I met Mrs. Cott for lunch at the Modern Museum. We ate upstairs in the members' dining-room and I noticed a lithograph on the hall walls where they display the rental collection by a Paul Waldman, born 1936. Wonder who *he* is—maybe he's the husband or brother of Diane at *Art News*. At least the prosaic old name is turning up in the arts a little nowadays, what with Frederic W. conducting the Musica Eterna and all that.

Jeremy Cott is both going and returning this summer on the same student ship as Carl. His mother got him a job through friends in an architect's office in London and he'll do surveying. He might decide to go into architecture himself. He saved his own passage money from that elevator job he had last year and he'll be getting a salary in London. Jon is trying to work out a way to go to Europe with Angelica for the summer, just to travel. They'd probably fly from out there directly as Mrs. C. will be abroad herself for 4½ months leaving the middle of April for Greece on a Greek ship and going to Israel and then up to northern Europe when the hot weather starts. The chances are, she thinks, that Jon will stay on at Berkeley and get a doctorate if only to stay out of the draft. He's already taking some courses in the doctoral program besides teaching. She and I went to several far-out art shows after lunch: Chryssa's (big jumbled metal type faces and neon light effects of ampersands, etc.) and Claes Oldenburg's (limp toilets bathtubs sinks urinals juicers potatoes fans cars) both terrifically clever and you should see them and the third by Tom Doyle (big curving bent shapes of some material like plywood but probably a plastic luridly colored which reminded me of objects put in sophisticated playgrounds for the kiddies to crawl through or stage sets for modern dance). We ended the afternoon at Mrs C.'s apt, where I saw a lot of the family snapshots around. Jon was such a cute kid. I took the Ashbery book along and showed it to her. Jon mentioned it when he called her last week but she hadn't seen it. She said he'd asked her to hunt through his cartons and find several short stories he once wrote and send them as he wants to submit them to a contest.

While I was writing this your check arrived and I'll attend to it.

Love & kisses,
Mummy

Noticed P. Scheldahjl having serious discussion with B. after getting his own papers back and heard him say, "Yes, but I'm very serious about what I'm trying to do . . ." B. kept apparently explaining something to him and he didn't look very happy—but then he has a sad face anyhow.

Mr. Boelitz is in hospital. Mrs. called but I haven't seen her.

Wednesday, 23 March 1966

Dear Annie,

Last night's poetry class started out slowly with only 4 people there at the beginning. This rather threw BB. He must have been wondering if he'd done something to lose them. He began reading from FINNEGANS WAKE and stumbling a lot and apologizing each time instead of just going on, which was a drag. But several more persons came and that perked him up. Even so the class was just about half size: me, Scheldahjl, Miss Mayer, Brownstein (the dark-haired slightly plump young guy who is usually with PS), Miss Myers, a couple of blondes and one nondescript dame.

After reading several sections from FW, about a page at a time, B. read two translations from the Odyssey, the part where Odysseus goes down to the dead. One was a prose translation, one was Alexander Pope's—which still stands up pretty well in spite of all the padding he did to make his heroic couplets. Then he read Pound's first Canto, which plunges right into the same incident but assumes the reader knows all about the situation so it's not a translation but an adaptation, of course. The discussion was too general, really, for me to report it very well. B. apparently is very much interested in the epic—maybe he is writing one. He even encouraged us, the class, to try our hand at epic stuff, using ancient myths as structures, though cautioning us to avoid silly anachronisms such as making Odysseus a U.S. merchant seaman lost getting back from Viet Nam. He also spoke of Pound's belief that at certain periods—the Homeric, or rather post-Homeric period, and the height of the Italian Renaissance—the language of mankind was pure, i.e. words had unmistakable meanings and men used them to say what they meant. P. also considered poets the guardians of the language, as well as the innovators for keeping it alive. We also discussed myths for a while. The reason B. reads so much to us, he said, is that he wants to get us to read all these things ourselves and keep on reading them. We should all, for instance, read Homer in as many different good translations as we can find, also Dante. And he can't imagine anybody's getting bored by FINNEGAN because it's so funny. It's also a good idea to take sections from Homer, Dante, etc. and rewrite or rework them ourselves, to get the feel of how to use language and maybe do something good. Perhaps I'll tackle something of the sort myself. Lately it's been hard for me to write again—I'm getting to learn more about poetry consciously and this can be inhibiting. Not that I'm giving up.

Glad Carl and Gregg had a good time, I'm expecting Carl home Friday or Saturday for his spring vacation.

Daddy and I both hope very much that you'll have the grace and tact to spend your birthday weekend here at home, even if you can't understand or admit any reason to. You'll have to take my word for it quite simply, if you won't see it yourself, that it is terribly important.

Love & kisses,
Mummy

Haven't been able to get another copy of POETRY with Ashbery's FRAGMENT, so please hang onto it and I'll copy it sometime.

Thursday, 24 March 1966

Dearest Annie,

Thanks very much for the poem. It's a good idea and the symbols are very apt, especially the pool. I agree about your last line and I also like the second stanza. I assume the two "theses" in the first line are typos for *these*. An interesting slip. You must be obsessed by the word *thesis* and the fact itself. I hope you do work over the poem. I've a few criticisms about grammar which I hope you won't resent. In verse 3, what does the first word *It* refer to? The dinner? Don't leave room for doubt. In verse 6, who are *They*? Who are *they* in 7 also? The first line of 8 might be better "Now I write to you about the event beforehand" and you can probably think of a still better way to put it. And in the last stanza, who has made the choice? A poem must be watertight and leave no question about whom or what the referents refer to unless the doubt is part of the whole concept. You often tend to use vague pronouns which sometimes seem right but sometimes they stop the flow of thought by being vague and asking for suspicion.

I don't think you should worry about such things at first writing, though, only while going over the poems afterwards.

Right now I'm just trying to carry out assignments for the class, I still haven't done the original one of a lot of one-line propositions but intend to try it for next week. Last Tuesday I turned in my 3-part assignment, consisting of 4 short couplets, one limerick, and ten lines in *terza rima*. (The limerick form B. specified, the other two forms were for us to choose.) The week before I turned in a long poem about the Sullivan St. *festa* called RITORNELLO. B. said it was too diffuse and he was right. He O.K.'d three of its stanzas, though. I'll work over it.

I'm sure meeting some of the Bennington alumnae helped start the poem in your mind. It suggests Vassar, too, and I daresay all the other institutions around the East.

Sunday evening Jean Boudin had us to dinner and she went with us to Shirley Broughton's for the two plays by George Stiles. Leonard Boudin stayed at home to work on the Julian Bond case—he has some 25 books of background reading, legal and historical, to get through fairly soon. Naturally he was interested in talking to Daddy about Speed Reading and what it can do. He's an interesting man, obviously brilliant. He was intrigued by hearing (from Jean) that we have such a beautiful daughter. Jean said he immediately thinks of any beautiful girl he hears about as a possible bride for their son Michael. She's very interesting herself—seems like a lost child with those big eyes and apparent confusion, yet she's terribly sharp and perceptive with an amazing memory—amazing because she doesn't remember things on the surface too well. She seems to operate on intuition rather than rational thought. The plays were pretty bad but the occasion was pleasant enough. Helen Eisner and her husband were there and we met other friends of theirs. Somebody ought to tell that Bennington Alumna Shirley Broughton what's happening in the theatre nowadays. Her tastes are unbelievably old hat or maybe she just lets other people come to her and ask her to let their plays be given but she'd better get wise. Her *forte* is getting top people to come and have discussions; she's very successful at that and those programs have always been fascinating—especially in that setting where there's a feeling of casual intimacy as contrasted with the big contrived affairs at the YMHA.

Yesterday passing through Gimbels' basement I saw that there was one of those English suits left which I've been admiring ever since you tried on a raspberry one around Christmas, which wasn't right at the shoulders for you. It always cost too much for me but this, the last one, was my size and color (bluey purpley) and down to $40 so how could I resist? Nice to suddenly have a way to acquire something one's wanted.

I ran into Dorothy Grotz and went home for tea with her. Her apartment looks so beautiful. She and Paul recently bought a lot of handsome modern chairs and a big dining table all made out of beautiful woods by a Japanese in New Hope, Pa. Dorothy wants me to write a detective story with her and I just may. She's going to London with Paul for the month of May and maybe we'll try it when they get back.

Glad you can hear Grebanier, if only to please Daddy. Bill Matthews played on CBS-TV recently and he came over very well indeed. He seems to be absolutely absorbed in his instrument and its sounds when he plays—actually suggests (to me) a mother bending over a wonderful baby. Daddy knows his father quite well. He was once a policeman and it was Grebanier who got him interested in education, or in going on with it, and he's been on the Pace faculty for years. He's musical himself to the extent of singing with the Oratorio Society, which gives a couple of concerts each year. Apparently Grebanier is one of those teachers who can really sometimes set some of his students on fire and change their lives. Paul Gray told me that's what happened to him.

Did I tell you Nina and Holland are taking a special class in how to prepare for and take auditions? Don't know the man's name who gives it. You seem to be enjoying your directing. Daddy always has thought you might be good at it. Is the tutorial with Gray?

Love & kisses,
Mummy

Monday, 11 April 1966

Dearest Annie,

I want to submit the enclosed poem to SILO. If you print it you can say, *Frances LeFevre lives in New York City. She is the mother of a Bennington senior.* I hope you do use it. I think it's good enough and then it's anti-war. Haven't shown it to Berkson yet. I don't have the original Greek so worked from two translations by MacNiece and Lattimore which I enclose for your information. As you see, I changed the emphasis and pushed the image of the money-changer because I think it's a strong one.

Yesterday Tom Griffin called and wished Daddy and me a happy Easter. He'd been in Washington for a week and said he was on his way to NY. I gather he would have liked to see you. His voice sounded very warm and strong and happy. I guess he's found his direction.

The other day a statement arrived from the Manufacturers Hanover Trust Company addressed to Miss Ann M. Waldman, at our address, so I got Mr. Knott on the phone and tried to straighten things out again. I also called Miss Ann M. W. and we had a chat. She's older, non-Jewish (she asked me if we were because of the spelling—as you know most non-Jews spell it with 2 *n*'s at the end—she didn't sound prejudiced though) and her father's family came from around Stuttgart but had lived in Czechoslovakia before they came here. (Her father's name is John, too!) Mr. Knott said that they did not succeed in tracing the one check you couldn't account for so I've called RVR and asked Miss Gould there to look up the cancelled ones and let me know, at her own convenience, what checks they have that were cleared through the MHTC. Probably it's all too confused to ever be straightened out but *if* there's $47 somewhere that belongs to you which you didn't get it's certainly worth a little effort. Too bad your own records are so spotty but how could you know this would happen.

Daddy's been simply miserable with his cold ever since you left and started taking antibiotics several days ago because his throat was hurting and he feared the flu. He spent the pre-Easter holiday in bed and seemed better today and went to work as usual. Marian Tracy, my friend who writes gourmet cook-books (she has about 12 in print) invited us for food yesterday afternoon but I went alone. Daddy was willing to go but I talked him out of it because he was too patently wretched. Marian's brother, Horace Coward, who's business manager of the Yale press, was there with his wife. They've a son who sounds a lot like Carl and has taken his junior year from Haverford abroad; right now he's just left Greece for Florence. His roommate at Hvfrd is David Lowry. There was another couple at Marian's—nothing unusual about the wife, but the husband's a TWA jet pilot (somehow I'd never expected to meet one!) who wants to study for the ministry. Seems he had some religious conversion experience a couple of years ago in Japan. Nothing wrong about that, I suppose, but he's all hung up on fundamentalism, Billy Graham approach or similar, and doesn't think the churches should be involved in psychiatry or social problems. How dreary, and wasteful. Otherwise he could do some good.

Did Carl get up to B'ington this last weekend?

Was looking over old issues of POETRY and in the double one for Oct.-Nov. 1963 found three more poems by Roethke, rather light verse: Supper with Lindsay, Song, and A Wheeze for Wystan. Do you want me to send them? If they're not in one of R.'s books the issue might be in your library (Vol. 103, Nos. 1 and 2).

How's the play going and when will it be? Should I come to see it? Do you need anything from here?

Love & kisses,
Mummy

Tuesday afternoon

Dear Annie,

I got Berkson on the telephone about what you said re his reading up there and told him to write you directly and tell you a couple of possible dates, preferably during the first two weeks in May, and the magazine would be glad to sponsor him if a time could be worked out. So you may be hearing from him. I also told him to send you two or three poems to tie in with his reading.

He asked about what arrangements there would be and I said no honorarium but hospitality and fare (he said plane, maybe? and I said I thought not and anyway the plane has to go to Albany). So he will look at his schedule and pick a couple of dates. If you have any difficulty about his fare you know you can count on me, anonymously of course. It isn't that much and I wouldn't want you and SILO to be embarrassed. He will very likely pick a weekend unless you know of some quick car or plane ride sometime other.

I'm about over this cold but it was a nuisance while it was at its peak.

Last night the operator wanted a call collect here from Carl to you confirmed so I assume he's planning to visit B'ington again next weekend when the parents invade Ham'ton. Daddy works Sat'days, you know, so we'll wait and probably go to see him during the football season sometime. If he comes up I hope he'll have a good time. Be helpful as you can.

Love & kisses,
Mummy

Come to think of it though, if the plane connections are good and the whole fare is under $25 perhaps it would be possible for BB? (If I helped SILO out?) I automatically said no to him simply because I never heard that people use the plane as a rule from NY. You will know better than I.

[This letter includes notes from Berkson's March 29 and April 12 classes, which Frances must have collected and sent with a letter a few days after her April 11 letter.]

Notes from Bill Berkson's Class

March 29 - *Modernism* really began in 15th century with high Renaissance.
  - is opposed to personal, highly romantic style, distinct from it.
  - is characterized by 3 abstract words: place, time, and history, all of which are used to contain and identify the *self.*
      e.g. Joyce in ULYSSES: Place—Dublin, Time—a day (in *FW* a night), History is expressed in J's awareness of time and place in particular and also generally—all time, all place.
  In the whole of 19th and 20th centuries there is great anxiety about self, place, and time. It's funny that now in both science and metaphysics place and time have suddenly jammed into one another (as in Einstein's, Minkowski's mathematics *et al*, where certain equations didn't prove workable unless *time* was included as a dimension and given value—this is my own addition for your enlightenment, M.)
  In *Finnegans Wake* practically every phrase shifts back and forth in place and time. Dublin was still like an 18th century town when Joyce grew up there. It had practically ignored all 19th century development of night life. In terms of language this mean the Dubliners spoke a language which was flooded with history buried in it, was radiant with it. Joyce felt the language to be on the one hand dead, riddled with clichés, on the other hand these very clichés embodied ideas, heroism, and elevations of the spirit which the 19th century destroyed almost completely for almost every other European country and language.
  2 things are common to 20th century art and literature: allusion & parody. They do not *reproduce* works of art but incorporate some essence of it in a new work. Parody does not necessarily make fun of art. Greek root is *para-odos*, by the road, something branching off in a new direction. Modern literature comes to a known thing, something known already, puts it into a new context and gives it a new meaning. The thing is usually parodied in *style* and *manner*. In Joyce, Pound,

Kafka, Mann, Ashbery, sometimes in Ginsberg, you have styles from other sorts of literature (Flaubert said, "Style is a way of thinking.") brought into contexts which either cancel the other styles, laugh them into another kind existence, or give them a new validity which history was beginning to deny them.

Joyce employs a kind of doubletalk using the language people speak showing what is vital and what is dead. Uses newspapers, of Dublin, England, France, where the evening tabloids (as here now in US) parody heroic eloquence (see Daily News). So Joyce parodies newspapers, uses music-hall melodramas—which have water-down elements of Aristotelian tragedy. In *FW* (as in Williams' *Paterson*) it's language which has *failed* the people, but it's only through language (the poet's) that they are reborn. In *FW* everything happens as *events in language*, only as WORDS. Take any sentence from *FW* and roll it around in your mind and put it back together again and you may succeed in pushing it toward a single meaning, but it's still the meaning of the *sentence*, not of any other reality.

(B. read "I Caught the Bird" of Thomas Nashe, from the Elizabethan Reader, as an example of a similar approach to language.)

Joyce's sentences express many different meanings, though, in terms of attitude. Many have an eloquent heroic manner and then something else will bring it down to burlesque and something else will turn it into an insult or a lie. All possibilities lie in words as they are made. J. uses a wrap-around style as opposed to usual meaning. His words and sentences are muscular and in-the-round, many-toned (with overtones too). Eliot called ULYSSES a book with many voices but no style.

The purpose of our reading Joyce: we can learn from him the modulation of language towards very hard very solid effects. How to orchestrate what we hear all around us in common life towards whatever effects we are out to achieve. In THE DUBLINERS the many romantic clichés are not just sentimental mush but really a true picture of the everyday life in which the language has failed people so much that they cannot even use it to find out what to make of their lives. See Molly Bloom's soliloquy.

Joyce makes words into solids that stand by themselves.

April 12 - BB opened by reading 4 poems, Hopkins's SPRING AND FALL: TO A YOUNG CHILD, Yeats's FISHERMAN (one of Pound's favorites) and LAPIS LAZULI and O'Hara's THE DAY LADY DIED (Lady being Billie Holiday, if you don't know). You have the Yeats but here are the other two (typing them out helps me to *get* them more, M.)

Hopkins: Márgarét, áre you gríeving

Over Goldengrove unleaving?
Leáves like the things of man, you
With your fresh thoughts care for, can you?
Ah! ás the heart grows older
It will come to such sights colder
By and by, nor spare a sigh
Though worlds of wanwood leafmeal lie;
And yet you wíll weep and know why.
Now no matter, child, the name:
Sórrow's spríngs áre the same.
Nor mouth had, no nor mind, expressed
What heart heard of, ghost guessed:
It ís the blight man was born for,
It is Margaret you mourn for.

★★★

O'Hara: It is 12:20 in New York a Friday
three days after Bastille day, yes
it is 1959 and I go get a shoeshine
because I will get off the 4:19 in Easthampton
at 7:15 and then go straight to dinner
and I don't know the people who will feed me

I walk up the muggy street beginning to sun
and have a hamburger and a malted and buy
an ugly NEW WORLD WRITING to see what the poets
in Ghana are doing these days

                        I go on to the bank
and Miss Stillwagon (first name Linda I once heard)
doesn't even look up my balance for once in her life
and in the GOLDEN GRIFFIN I get a little Verlaine
for Patsy with drawings by Bonnard although I do
think of Hesiod, trans. Richmond Lattimore or
Brendan Behan's new play or *Le Balcon* or *Les Nègres*
of Genet, but I don't, I stick with Verlaine
after practically going to sleep with quandariness

and for Mike I just stroll into the PARK LANE
Liquor Store and ask for a bottle of Strega and
then I go back where I came from to 6th Avenue
and the tobacconist in the Ziegfeld Theatre and
casually ask for a carton of Gauloises and a carton
of Picayunes, and a NEW YORK POST with her face on it

and I am sweating a lot by now and thinking of
leaning on the john door in the 5 SPOT
while she whispered a song along the keyboard
to Mal Waldron and everyone and I stopped breathing

    (Think I begin to understand O'Hara better now. He didn't
bewilder me but I read him hastily and didn't see the depths.)
    Then we discussed them, BB asking the usual what have the 3
poems in common what difference.
    All have eloquence in common, they illuminate speech.
    At first reading Hopkins and Yeats sound more dramatic, at second
reading you (should) realize they are more conversational compared to
O'Hara. While O'Hara's poem seems to be a rush of chatty, colloquial
name-dropping, and then you see it's more rhetorical than the other

two—he's making a statement on a high level (Billie Holiday that marvelous gift of life has gone out of the crummy world she could transfigure for people sometimes.)

O'Hara's technique is a series of punch lines you think are describing personal everyday experience then suddenly they take you out into abstract speculation and turn into something marvelous (or tell you something marvelous has happened). O'H. is neither oratorical nor intimate but sounds as if making a confession of a sort he might make to friends at a party. Yeats is more oratorical but still sounds more intimate. Hopkins, for all the more obvious formality of the poem, is the most intimate of all—talking to a single person.

Yeats has a trick (specially in LAPIS LAZULI) of moving you very far intellectually and emotionally, and then you realize the content is actually crazy, or silly, but then this is what poetry *is* (outside the everyday supposedly rational life, etc.) The poem is like OZYMANDIAS in the desert, it is just *there*. Joan Crawford's old movies have the same quality (this I don't know about, do you? M.). They approximate the square root of the sublime, that is to say in the religious sense of being mystical, super-moving. Plato wanted to set up his Republic of men who all were reasonable, who knew their function and carried it out. But in reality this is impossible for you always get the poets too, who question things and answer them only in a sense that does not *translate* very well into mundane talk.

BB made a slip several times on the word sublimity—said *subliminy*. Much laughter.

He also gave a terrific imitation of Yeats reading THE LAKE ISLE OF INNISFREE, which he knows from an actual recording. I'm sure it was very much like WBY—it must have been. We all applauded.

For the future we are to read all the Williams we can, he'll wind up on Joyce and do a class on Williams. Also read a number of sonnets, Milton on his blindness, some of Shakespeare, Michael Drayton, Keats, and think about what the word *sonnet* means as form and try to write a poem expressing what we think about this. The sonnet demands a certain way of thinking *inside* a poem in a very short space and the thought may take off in severely opposite or parallel directions even within a single line. It's a way or manner of thinking that pushes toward condensation and we all can profit from condensation, he said, unless we really *need* to write sprawlingly.

Hoey (the man on the other side of me the time you were there) asked why so many poets use the *sock in the last line*—he said it seems to be a syndrome and does it have to be that way? He asked why a poem cannot be a "field" that just drifts into reality occasionally. His "field" was not explored much, but BB said:

> Grand starts almost always come out of some perception of how to use casual everyday rhetoric. The thrust on the page gives immediacy.

> Ashbery often builds a poem between a big first line and a big last line. A powerful last line tends to provide a release *out* of the tension the poem builds up. Scheldahjl at this point volunteered that THE SKATERS ends inconclusively and started reciting. (I've the feel that there's something abject and creepy about *his* admiration of Ashbery, as if it were unthinking worship. Between you & me, I think some of the great A. is marvelous and exciting and beautiful, but *sometimes* my mind does wander, as it does with most of them, even Pound and Shakespeare! And Scheldahjl doesn't seem to have much humor and looks so *sad* and ashen all the time. I'd like to put him under a sun lamp for a couple of hours. M.) FELIX RANDALL is a good example of a casual beginning.

(B. said—Some, many, people writing today think if they've a good first line and a good last one anything will go between. This of course is from not *having* anything to put there, really.)

★★★★

Well, dear Annie, now you can catch up with what I'm learning and I hope it may be useful to you. Your letter has just arrived, nice to get it. I see that I was hasty in assuming I'd missed the only chance to see the play. If they decide to do it again let me know and I'll try to come up unless you are sure (not just shy or modest) that it wouldn't be worth the trip. But I wouldn't mind the trip. I could come up the same day and take the late bus back, perhaps, as Nina did.

I wish Carl knew how to be more aggressive with girls. But it's not his fault if there aren't many that meet his standards. He told me that of all the girls he's known the only one he can imagine himself married to is Gay, though naturally he is not considering marriage for a long time. Probably he would like a long love affair with someone he'd probably marry eventually. I don't think he's the type to enjoy brief encounters particularly. Well, it's mainly a matter of luck and chance. I suppose G. considers him too young, though *she* seems young and nobody else thinks that important. He thinks she's afraid of involvement, I don't think he'll mind my telling you this because you must have an idea of it yourself and he's probably said much the same to you. And I shall not say anything to anyone else.

Last night Berkson caught up with me on the street after class and said, "How's Anne?" I told him you'd been directing a play, he asked whose, etc. Then he said he'd really like to go up to Bennington and hoped you could arrange something and he'd be glad to do a reading there. Can you? I'm sure he'd give you something for SILO if he came. Will you either write me or call me about this before next Tuesday so I can tell him then and find out when *he* could go. He is such a dandy. Last night he was wearing a navy blue jacket, obviously new, with brass buttons. And some of his ties are very loud-arty. Have you ever read the long poem of O'Hara's in the CONTROVERSY OF POETS? It's dedicated to B. and is I guess a love poem to him. Another of O'H.'s in LUNCH POEMS also dedicated to him has the epigraph from D.H. Lawrence, "One or another / Is lost, since we fall apart / Endlessly, in one motion depart / From each other." They are I must say pretty public about their feelings. BB's face is quite handsome sometimes as he reads and he doesn't have a fairy voice at all—he has a very beautiful voice most of the time unless he's rattled by something like people dropping out of class (some are back but others have gone so it's about half the original number). His voice is much better than Ashbery's!

Daddy and I listened together to Donald Gardiner's reading on RVR last night. The radio's beginning to conk out again and he muffled his words deeply, from shyness I presume. But we still heard quite a bit and I can tell he's a poet, not a pretender.

It was inconsiderate of your typewriter not to hold out till you graduated. Surely there is a general typewriter repair place in Bennington, though. Do take it for an estimate and we'll be glad to pay anything under $25. If it's irreparably broken why don't you rent one at the same place until your thesis is done? You remember Daddy used to rent one in Millville for $10 a month, probably $15 now but still . . . I'll help you get a new one, or maybe give you one for your graduation present, but try to see what can be done until June. I'd sort of like to hang on to the little Olivetti as a spare, or at least find out what it would fetch as a trade-in down here. What could you get for it at the college if it's broken? Incidentally if you rent one we'll pay the charge.

I wore my new bluey-purpley English suit for the first time to a tea yesterday afternoon and love it. The weather's been so cold that I've continued to wear my new coat, the one you saw, quite a lot. Fun!

"Bird Bath" given somewhere around here recently, perhaps at LA MAMA, am not sure. Kevin O'C. was in it but not Barbara. Seems unfair. I think of it as *her* play. But then there may have been reasons of her own. I saw "Chicago" and I think it was with Gay. Have you heard from Simone? I worry about her but I don't think I should call her without a really good extra-curricular reason.

Don't forget to let me know about Berkson. I'll speak to Scheldahjl and Bernadette Mayer next week, casually, yes, about SILO.

Love & kisses,
Mummy

Wednesday, 20 April 1966

Dear Annie-pie,

Got your letter, glad to hear etc. especially that Simone is OK. Naturally the thought had entered my head that her other complications *might* be causing the symptoms and luckily it was so. And I remembered a similar incident concerning Randa several years ago; funny, Simone was around then, that night we were having a big dinner party here. Well, psychoses or not I still hope the girls get more careful—real babies are far from being just fun and games. And abortions are a crummy business and quite expensive nowadays, though no more so relatively speaking than they were during the depression, when for many it was a terribly desperate matter to raise the $50 or $100 they cost then. I'd like to see S. straighten out. My impression is that she's basically a simple elemental female who'd be quite happy as a French housewife with some cultural interests but not too many. She has always seemed to me to be out of her depth, trying to be something she is not. This is primarily a social question—I don't mean this in a snobbish sense, I mean she hasn't been thrown with the types of people she'd do better with, and this can louse anybody up who is not aggressive or realistic or shrewd about such matters.

Ezra Pound is quoted in one of his biographies as saying that it's vitally important for a poet to have a social sense and be able to "place" people in the way that a brilliant hostess does.

Thanks for the suggestion about sending THE SIBYL, but at this stage I'm not satisfied with any of the translations I ever did and have also lost interest in Angelos, at least for the moment. That's why I never sent the MS of the shortened version to Cyril Peters. I still might do something with it. Frankly, what stops me most is the typing. If I had a secretary or, better still, a *slave* who could type endlessly, everything would be fine and I'd be a lot more productive. My perfectionism is also a factor that limits me, but I wouldn't give that up for anything. I do believe the real poets have to be perfectionists about every word. Of course I understand how you feel about writing—once it becomes a compulsion you're really lost to most of the other things people take so seriously, yet at the same time everything is enhanced for you. You can see why I've resisted writing for most of my life, though. You, anyway, have other abilities and assets that will help you cope and, with luck, you can use them all and write, too.

I stopped at the 8th St. Bkstre and got MAGAZINE. I already knew your poem, of course, but it's nice to see it in print. It's so much better than anything else in the issue except the piece on Spicer's *Language*—they are the only things worth reading. I am very weary of what has apparently become a convention on many levels of the avant-garde—every poem must mention at least one of the following (a) shit, (b) the rectum, (c) the toilet (d) the toilet's flushing, (e) fucking, preferably homosexual. Happily, this does not apply on every level. On the highest and most sophisticated levels (Ashbery, Koch, Auden, Levertov, the academics) the sexual and cloacal are used if they fit into the poem integrally but they aren't made quite as much of. Naturally, even the big boys still have their little moments of fun occasionally; but we will not deny them those as long as they've all the other stuff too. I think subtlety in expressing these subjects—hints, allusiveness, symbols—is much more interesting and *then* when bald statement becomes inevitable it is much more to the point.

Monday, 25 April 1966

Dearest Annie,

I'm mailing you a box of clothes today. Picking out what to send has been pure guesswork and I've probably missed some of the things you really wanted. But I can always send more. I've included your replacement present from the Brooklyn Museum—hope you like it— and a pair of white net stockings and a late birthday present from Nina T., who came down here to dinner last evening. (It's in the tiny box.) Her address, if you haven't it, is 19 W. 82 St.

Carl's OK, doesn't seem to be too depressed about anything. Probably because he's got his trip abroad to focus on. He's stuck pretty close to the house studying as he brought a lot of homework with him. He'll be here till tomorrow afternoon since he has enough cuts to use up.

Saturday night I went to a party given by Jean Boudin and Helen Eisner at the Eisners' house on Waverly Place. It was partly a money-raising and discussion affair for one of the conscientious objectors whose case Leonard B. is handling through the Emergency Civil Liberties Committee and was very interesting. There must have been over a hundred and twenty-five people there, including a lot of young ones. Met the Eisners' son John who goes with a B'ington sophomore, Alexa Davis. He said he's heard lots about you, up there *and* in the Village (what, I wonder? I couldn't tell.) Helen Eisner's play, which was to be done soon by one of those loft groups, has been put off till the fall. Jean had invited several people from her poetry workshop, whom I met, of course, and I also saw several old friends to talk to. Had a nice time.

Yesterday afternoon Marianne Moore was scheduled to read at the Loeb Center, NYU, and I went, and it was both moving and saddening because it was obviously too much for her. She is nearly 80, you know, and sort of frail physically,—not sick, but she hasn't much endurance. The reading fell apart very soon—she would start talking and rambling about the poems and there was no telling which was which. Also she'd tell about a poem she was about to read and them fumble around her papers and be unable to find it and say she must have left it at home—

this happened several times. The audience was huge—that rather large auditorium (where we heard Lowell once) was about ¾ full and I think the size of it was one of the things that threw her—she was pleased and excited about it and couldn't calm down sufficiently to function. It's her memory that's disorganized, for she is still writing, and she got off quite a few witty remarks spontaneously. After it had become evident that she couldn't handle the reading the chairman took over and suggested that the audience ask questions, and the affair then became a sort of conspiracy between him and the audience to keep things going as long as possible— he would re-phrase the questions to make them easy for her and add his own comments when she started getting shaky in her answers. Even some of the questions were too much, like when a girl asked her what modern poets she liked and she started talking about one and then she couldn't remember his name, only that he's published by Knopf. But she rallied wittily enough and said, "Well, Mr. Knopf will be glad to supply his name." The audience of course was totally sympathetic and gave her enormous applause at the end, and a whole big crowd went up for autographs afterwards. We've our own autograph, you know, the letter she wrote Daddy (recently he had it framed and hung it up himself in the dining room!). Much was made of the fact (by the chairman) that she has moved to the Village (9ᵗʰ St.) from Bklyn.

Lowell is reading at the Loeb at 4:15 Thursday and at 8:30 the same evening Ashbery is reading at St. Mark's Church. (Bet that he will be mobbed.) Don't know if I'll get to the first but I certainly intend to go to the second. Coincidentally, Ashbery's poetry is scheduled on RVR Thursday night and his and your little magazine discussion for Friday, at least according to the old schedule I have. Cyril never kept his promise to send me the new one, which is a nuisance.

Nina finally broke with Angelo two weeks ago. His position was that their affair had not progressed enough to make him want marriage and he had too high an opinion of her to ask her to go on without commitment, etc. Her opinion is different because she felt she could be a good wife and give him what he needs and wanted to marry him. But, she says, she realizes she made a mistake in coming over to be near him and making herself too available—she can see how he started backing away from her gradually even then—the old, old story. *I* think *he's* the loser, not she, but I guess he was a lot better than the others she has been close to marrying, and she hasn't yet met anybody else around here who appeals to her. She says there are so many homos in her office—she is repelled by them but also would like to know what makes them the way they are. In Athens, apparently, they don't hang around normal social groups very much but have their own world. Recently at a party a young Lesbian was really going after her—she sensed it right away, but managed to avoid giving her her phone number. The Greek Easter, which was the same as ours this year (they coincide every 7 years I believe), she went down to Washington to spend with Elly and Bob, and Angelo went down too in what he himself thought was a graceful gesture because she had invited him before they had decided to part. But it spoiled it for her. Angelo went off by himself much of the time and appeared only for meals, except for one conversation with her upstairs while everybody else was having a good time feasting in the garden—(Elly had all the Easter works and foods and drinks and lots of people)—and he actually broke down during this, as he's done before. A strange guy. She's probably well out of it, though she won't think so unless and/until something better happens. She doesn't want to tell her parents yet that the affair with A. has come to nothing—it will hurt them because she has been hurt, she says, and it will be easier to tell them casually when she's home this summer. She is going over for July and part of August, most of the time with the Weinbergs' dig in Israel. Did you know she has been taking Hebrew at Hunter 2 evenings a week? She told me, too, that she is now regretting she has not done more with her life, studied more, etc. (I told her she's done a lot more than most girls I know just the same, which is true, certainly, with respect to her jobs and her special skill.) She is looking into courses at the Institute of Interior Design, as a possibility for the future if she comes back here in the fall. She's not sure yet, but her boss at Harrison & Abramowitz will keep her job for her. She looks so lovely—all this has made her lose weight—but she is sad and disillusioned and can't enjoy anything except momentarily. However she says she knows this will pass.

The last contemporary music concert of the season is at the McMillan tonight and Jean Howard, who's my regular pal for these affairs, and a fun one too, is going with me. Daddy and I had expected to go to a play reading at Shirley Broughton's studio last Friday, Brecht's "Edward II", with James Earl Jones and others, but still felt knocked out by our 2 colds and besides Carl was coming home, so we passed that one up. How is Culture doing in your area these days? Are they going to repeat Alan's play? Carl told me about it and it sounded fine— he said you know how to handle actors pretty well. I still hope to see it sometime.

Love & kisses,
Mummy

[undated, probably April 25 or 26 1966]

The effect of the poetry workshop on me so far is to make me much more critical and attentive in everything I read. I'm also getting more exacting with myself than ever before (and it was bad enough as it was) and although I'm writing a little more often, and certainly more regularly, it's becoming really maddening not to do still more and much better. My poems are a lot tighter, which I think is good, although I never was a sprawly writer—which the majority of the class seem to be and BB thinks they should pull some of it together more. Lately I've been concentrating on the assignments—like an Elizabethan sonnet, which was fun to do.

Last evening's session was spent again on the nature of language, as Flaubert perceived it and tried to fight its decay. BB read a couple of short sections from the novel *Bouvard et Pécuchet* (Daddy had brought it home and was talking to you about it when you were here, if you remember, so I was really *up* on things). Here are the points he made:

Wallace Stevens called poetry "the supreme fiction", i.e, it's an artifact, not quite real or necessary in any functional sense.

Fiction in the 18th and 19th centuries had become completely contrived and sentimental—there was an unbelievable flood of bad works of fiction and even the better-written ones were sentimental.

Flaubert (and others) began to realize that the whole system (of values, of existential implications, of approaches to conduct, of taste and standards) expressed by this type of fiction had corrupted the real lives of European people and made *them* artificial. Even men and women who were not themselves readers were affected by all this and lived their lives and made their decisions accordingly.

Flaubert wrote *Madame Bovary* to show the effect on a simple woman of thinking (erroneously) that her life would not be complete unless she experienced a grand romantic love affair, and she set about accordingly to louse up what she did have that was good. (Maybe this is Simone's type of problem.)

Together with the phony sentimentality *Flaubert* also despised the 18th century intellect, the cataloguing mind that thinks disconnected facts and trivia are the height of knowledge, the encyclopedia lover. *Bouvard et Pécuchet* is the story of two simple-minded accountants who meet, acquire an inheritance to live on, and decide to devote their lives to assembling all the knowledge of the human race. It's a satire, of course, and has been compared to Joyce's works, especially *Ulysses*, because J. also was aware of the futility of the mind that's not able to do more than collect isolated facts and he too satirizes it and at the same time tries frantically to pack all knowledge into his books.

Hugh Kenner has a recent book FLAUBERT, JOYCE, BECKETT: *The Stoic Comedians* about this whole question, I'm reading it now and recommend it for when you've some time. It's very short.

Difference between Flaubert and Joyce: F. hated the people he satirized, found nothing redeeming them. Joyce burlesqued them and their speech beautifully and accurately and often devastatingly but always with warmth. He forgave them; Flaubert could not, Leopold Bloom with all his weaknesses was shown to be a good man in Molly's soliloquy, etc.

Berkson then read "The Triumph of Dullness" (from line beginning *In vain in vain the all-composing hour,* to, *Universal Darkness buries all.*) from Pope's DUNCIAD, which I am sure you must know, telling us to mark particularly the couplets' constructions, half-line working against half-line, line against line, parallel and opposing thoughts and qualities, place of the caesura, etc, etc.

Next he read two sections from A SEASON IN HELL (Rimb.): "Bad Blood" and "A Night in Hell": parts of a poem on the bathtub in Auden's ABOUT THE HOUSE (he likes some of Auden) and of Koch's "The Seine"; and some notes on Poetics in Valéry's Selected Writings, which I don't have.

Then he said he was going to go around the class (about 8-10 were there) and ask us all one by one to tell what *presuppositions* are in our minds when we sit down to begin writing a poem. He admitted afterwards that he had failed to express clearly what he wanted—maybe he hated to make it easy or something. What he *wanted*, and explained afterwards, was our presuppositions about the nature of language and the rules we have to follow to use it effectively. You can see that all his discussions of Joyce, Flaubert, are related to this. (Daddy is really amazed that we talk so much about fiction—he thought poetry was something entirely apart.) Naturally, what happened, since he hadn't made this clear enough, was that everybody talked about himself: "My levels of consciousness", "My communication with others", "My feeling that my poem will *work*". "My feelings about the world"—you have heard it all. None of it was bad or offensive but it was all meaningless. Of course you know me, I tossed my part off lightly and said my only presupposition is that I'm going to be surprised, maybe pleasantly maybe not, which got a laugh. BB took me up on this philosophically so I had to expand it a little and said of course I start with the person I am, conditioned and limited by circumstance and experience and all that but there is still always a surprise . He kept at it but still not getting his point across about language and I finally told him I supposed my only basic presupposition was that I'd be alive long enough to finish the poem. SO next week's assignment is supposed to make us think about presuppositions and develop more understandings. This is how he put it:

PRESUPPOSITIONS:
"You accept the language that is spoken around you and that you speak."
"You deal with it in writing."
"The way you write will reflect what you think those words do—what effects they have, what effects they can be permitted to have—how you can change the effects they are known to have to what you want them to have."
"You assume that your readers understand the language."
"You can assume the existence of a large, widely accepted set of rules. You can also *not* assume or accept it."

  Assignment: Write a poem, or series of poems, in which every noun refers either to a female person, object, or abstraction of either, or to a male ditto, and every verb is an indication or sign of either positive affectionate behavior or negative hostile behavior. The entire language of you and your audience with respect to your poem or poems is based on your words being what the language is.

He still didn't satisfy the class with his clarity and I've no idea how I'm going to work this out yet. It seems to be an arbitrary decision he's asking for, because he said for instance we might say that all words having 3 or more consonants are masculine. It would be so much easier to write this one in French or Greek! But I dimly see the point he wants to make is that we always accept and abide by some rules whether we know it or not. *C'est ici une véritable mystique du langage, n'est-ce pas?*

I came across these ghastly A.B.L. poems the other day while looking for something else and being pre-occupied for half a second I thought they were yours—the initials were perfectly familiar (my mother's) and also resembled A.L.W. so my mind took a slightly uncanny flip (ghost writing!) until I read the letter. What a sad sack and creep, poor guy.

Miss Gould at Riverside called me and said that only one of your checks was ever cleared through Manufacturers Hanover and that was on March 2. The others, all of them, you cashed at a savings bank or banks. She sent me a photostat of the Mar. 2 one which obviously is of no help to you whatever but I didn't tell her that and thanked her properly and warmly. I suppose if you want to check all the rest you can go up there sometime. They have them all, so nothing was lost. They issued ten checks to you altogether, she said. Is there anything else you can do?

I'll knock off now and traipse up the avenue to the post office and mail this and also the payment for Carl's passage, which has come due. Carry on!

Love & kisses
Mummy

Tuesday night, April 26 1966

Dear Annie-pie,

Not much to report from this evening's class as BB mostly read poems by class members and discussed them. Some of the issues that came up were interesting, as the use of color in poetry, which he's against for the most part, This caused some consternation among the more visual-minded people present, who almost think of a poem as a painting and mention green here, orange there, pink somewhere else, all in isolation as if they were dabs of pigment. BB says it's all right to mention color if it's an integral part of a description, or of an object you want to specify, and the great color line of all time is "the dawn in russet mantle clad", but otherwise he thinks it's likely to be a false note and slow the poem down. He also warned us that it's almost impossible for you to convey your own visual image or memory to anyone else linguistically, whether you're telling a story or describing what someone else wore or whatever. He said try telling something funny you saw just by describing it as a picture and it'll fall flat unless you also employ some tricks of language or narration, like wit, suspense, quotation, contrast, irony. Various people gave him an argument—Schjeldahl (I finally think this is the way to spell it!) brought up Koch's constant use of color, but BB defended that by pointing out KK's tricks. BB said *he* thinks the "yellow fog" in Prufrock is one of the most unpleasant uses of color in all poetry and he'd like to see it deleted. Hannah Weiner, (who was recently in Paris, knows Ashbery, took the Fugs' record to Paris, etc.) was crushed and kept protesting that she can't write about anything else but color, and BB suggested that she might really be a painter. He wasn't nasty in any of his comments. The class has apparently become stabilized with people who get on with him and understand what he's driving at, so it's a warmer atmosphere lately. He read a sonnet I'd written as an exercise the week he told us to read some sonnets and try to get inside their language.

He said he liked it a lot—his words were "actually I'm rather fond of it," so naturally I was pleased. Hoey and Schjeldahl, however, put up a ridiculous and unnecessary argument about the futility of writing sonnets at all—S. went on and on about it and he *whines* so when he talks in class, although they knew, if they were listening (maybe they weren't!) that I'd written it as an exercise. Anyway, at one point BB said, "*If* any of you think that it is *not* a useful and valuable ability to be able to write poetry in a variety of forms there is something lacking in you, and I'll be glad to disabuse you of this notion if you wish me to. We need a race of poets with the skill and sophistication to turn out whatever form of poetry might be assigned to them. It even takes a considerable amount of skill to write the lyrics for a popular song." One of the first things he said to me when he came in was, "I liked all your new poems—they're all so different—each one is by a different person—if there's anything I hate it's consistency!" One that he gave back was the Agamemnon thing I sent you—he suggested a couple of changes, but I don't entirely agree with them all, or haven't thought them out yet, at least. He thinks I should put something more colloquial, a quoted speech perhaps, instead of "No answer comes." He said it was good and interested him very much and made him want to sit down and start writing a version of his own. I don't expect SILO to use it, but if they, or you, should, in some burst of generosity or just possibly an appreciation of old Greeks and modern mothers, let me know in case I want to make any change.

BB read a little Williams and the very first poem was called "To Elsie."

I'd never seen or heard it, as it's only in the large volume of the collected works, but as he read it I realized that it was about Elsie Orahley, the teenage orphan who spent a year with Ann Harris's family in Wildwood early in the 20s and ran wild and left behind her a copy of THE NEW POETRY inscribed to her by Dr. Williams in 1923, which Ann still has and showed me last summer. In the book are also a couple of snapshots of WCW holding his two small sons. Elsie had lived with the Williams family the year before, helping out with the children. After BB had finished I said I knew who Elsie was and I told the class the story, so he read the poem a second time. It's quite interesting— WCW had a very sensitive and compassionate feeling about her and her situation and the way she was probably going to turn out—she must have been 15 when he wrote it. I'll try to find the book in the library and copy it and show it to you sometime. Or it may be at B'ington, too.

I never did my assignment for this week—the one in which we were to set up arbitrary genders for nouns and meanings for verbs, but I'm glad I didn't because BB explained it more carefully to those who were absent last week and I see now that it was just supposed to be a device for us ourselves, to help us look at words and their shades of meaning differently—the aim being to help us dissociate more easily. BB wrote on the board two lines by

Pasternak:

The wind rushes headlong.
The sea washes the headland.

Suppose, he said, that you arbitrarily decide all nouns with two or more consonants are masculine (wind, headland) and all verbs containing an "a" are an expression of hostility, and all verbs without "a" show affection. You can make these decisions any way you choose. Then with this in mind you look at these two sentences and their meaning, or effect, changes from what it had seemed at first: "rushes" becomes a gentle motion and "washes" a violent one. And so on. It's just another trick of the far-outs, I guess, to keep shaking the old rigid concepts apart and try new effects. Next week we're going to be told some of the ways of picking up people's speech and breaking it up into poetic phrases and lines, Williams was one of the masters at that and BB suggested we read a lot of him aloud to ourselves.

After I came home I listened to Schjeldahl's reading on RVR. He sounded OK and the poems were pretty good—some better than others. He's so deadly serious about himself, though. He's having something in the next Art & Lit.

BB said to me he hadn't written you yet because he's uncertain about his time in relation to things coming up at the Museum.

Carl left this afternoon by bus. He's going to try to get up to B'ington at least once more, to see you before he goes off to Europe (June 7), unless you'll both get home sometime on the same weekend. He can't make any plans for his birthday weekend until he knows when he has to take that goddamned Selective Service test—they assign a specific date for it. He called Mark to try to get his advice about marketing David Campbell's songs—he's written over a hundred, both lyrics and music, and Carl says some of them are beautiful. I'm sure Mark will help if he can. I haven't seen him or his family since March but we speak often. Mr. and Mrs. Boelitz are about to take a driving trip down through the Blue Mountains, into Kentucky, Tennessee and Georgia. Mrs. B. plans to visit some weaving places, including my friend Mary Hambidge's in Georgia.

I guess the trip to Libya has been dropped—I didn't ask. Martin wants them to come out to California in July, when he'll have his vacation. Mr. B. is feeling at least well enough for this trip, so I hope they can count on a decent interval before his trouble recurs—evidently the best they can hope for is these periods of remission.

You've never told me what you decided to do about your typewriter. Are you keeping it to have it fixed here? As I told you, I think we should hang onto it for a spare, since our other spares are in poorer shape than it is, I'm sure. I'm not completely satisfied with this and should take it for some adjustment but I can't live without it. So if yours is put in shape and is around I can borrow it temporarily.

Love & kisses,
Mummy

Thursday, 28 April 1966

Dearest Annie,

Daddy brought a Williams volume home for me from the Pace library, so here's the Elsie Orahley poem. I really think Williams is one of the greatest—not of all time, but of this country and its first half-century, particularly in his PATERSON. Daddy has been reading him and really "gets" a lot of it. You must be getting awfully tired of Roethke at this point but don't put him down for good—he certainly was one of the best in writing about the self, better than Lowell, I'd say, though I enjoy a lot of Lowell's devices.

No date's given anywhere that I can find for TO ELSIE, but it must have been written early in the twenties around the time she was with the Williamses or after she went to Wildwood. I wonder if she ever saw it; probably not. Evidently Williams tried to educate her a little since he gave her THE NEW POETRY. Ann Harris told me she liked to recite verses. But she didn't take the book with her.

I've just received your new poem and it's beautiful. I'm afraid of saying the wrong thing if I comment further, so do just take my word for it that I love it and feel very much pleased that you sent me a copy,

Hope I can get up to see the play if you do it again.

I'm going to the Cunningham ballet, SUMMERSPACE, Sunday afternoon with Marian Tracy. The reviews were all raves, so I'm sure it's worth seeing. A recital by Cunningham and company at the Brooklyn Academy of Music got even bigger raves—"a disgrace that there should be only one performance by this company this whole season", etc. Totty West Sullivan told me Cunningham is thinking of disbanding his company altogether and taking off for Europe because of the lack of support here. Dancers seem to have it harder than almost anyone else in the arts.

Such nasty wet chill weather again that I've felt my cold might be coming back. It had better not before tonight as I do want to get to hear Ashbery. Seems this type of cold comes from a particular virus and has been prevalent enough to be written about—it hangs on unusually long, leaves one dragged out for a while afterwards—which has been true with Daddy and me both. Also it's dangerous and even fatal to babies. Well, we're trying to take care of ourselves and get over it and not spread it any more than we can help. Keep well yourself, up in that healthful air!

Love & kisses,
Mummy

Saturday morning

Dearest Annie,

Ever since you decided to write on Roethke I've been keeping my eyes open for a copy of NEW WORLD WRITING 19 which has the symposium on "In A Dark Time" including the poet's own comments. I had quite given up on it but yesterday I had a few extra moments on my way to meet Dona and Lou at the Americana Hotel and I dropped into a Paperback Gallery at B'way & 50th and there it was. Perhaps it's too late to be of any real use to you but maybe not. Anyway I'm rushing it to you. Thought Chuck Stein might call about your things but he never did; I could have sent it with him if he were going up.

Thursday Jean Boudin and her friend Helen Eisner (who writes plays) came here to lunch and to hear the Sam Shepard tapes. What with their arriving late and the inevitable chitchat we didn't have time for both, just "Icarus", but we all enjoyed that. I had waited for them to come to listen to it myself. We all felt that by hearing it together and discussing it, and especially by being able to play back parts that weren't altogether clear to one or another of us at first we got a great deal more out of it than by just hearing it alone or reading it. Jean almost brought Marin Riley along but she and Bob were going to the Cape for the weekend. Marin has never seen any of Shepard's plays and has been hearing about him and is interested. She may read for the play of Helen's that's being given soon, as one of the actresses has had to leave the cast.

Wednesday evening Marjorie Sickels invited me to a performance of "The Lady's not for Burning" by a group at the Church of the Heavenly Rest. I'd never seen any Christopher Fry or even read anything by him. I enjoyed it though it seemed pretty irrelevant. The actors were amateurs or maybe semi-pros, some of them, but they were lively and high-spirited and there was a nice quality to the whole atmosphere—enthusiastic audience, etc. The only one I didn't care for was the heroine—the Lady accused of witchcraft.

I telephoned Long Island U. for information on that writers' conference and yesterday 5 brochures arrived in the mail all at once, several addressed to me with different versions of my name and different house numbers, and even one for Carl. In the same mail were 3 identical announcements from the NY Shakespeare Festival, 3 from the Poetry Center (Russian translations coming up next) and 2 inviting me to join an Indian dance class on the West coast. Crazy! The only session at LIU which appeals to me is a small discussion for writers and LIU students next Saturday morning at 10:00 conducted by Saurraute and Butor. But to go to it one has to register for the whole conference at a cost of $15; it is not open to the general public as the big meetings are, with single admission at 2.50. Since nothing else appeals to me I've decided to forget it. Those large general discussions serve little purpose except to give nobodies a chance to see what the somebodies look like. They're even having one general meeting on the question "Do Writers' Conferences Serve Any Purpose?" or words to that effect. Which is surely a ploy within a ploy!

We are going to hear Marshall McLuhan, though. He is speaking at the YMHA on May 7th and we've already sent for tickets, Daddy and I, as we think it may be a sellout. I've not heard of his having spoken publicly here before though he may have done so before anybody had heard of him much.

Today is Daddy's morning teaching at Pace Westchester and I'm following him up there later so we can spend the afternoon and early evening with Phyllis Jacoby in Pleasantville. Knud and Annette Stouman will be there also. Annette was the one I knew slightly at Vassar and she and Phyllis were on the boat I first went to Europe on, etc. Knud is Danish and writes books on public health. Tomorrow evening we're going to see two one-act plays at Shirley Broughton's studio. Jean Boudin and Helen Eisner will be there also.

Saw Robert Duncan on a Channel 13 program but he didn't come over as impressively as in real life—looked rather heavy—I don't mean physically. And these programs murder poetry. Radio is much better.

Love & kisses,
Mummy

Did Jim Rooney reach you? Called the other day and asked for your number. He's worn himself out running Club #47 he said and is going to Greece for 3 weeks in May to rest—Lucky.

Saturday

Dearest A.,

We listened to you on RVR last night and thought the discussion pretty good. It was probably much better than it seemed to you when you were in the midst of it. Your voice was fine and your questions all pertinent—Daddy was impressed. The few uhs and ahs did not obtrude because everybody else had them—some a lot more than you. We really enjoyed the whole thing. Am about to go shopping with Nina T. She needs spring clothes and I'm going to introduce her to Klein's.

Much love,
Mummy

Wednesday, 4 May 1966

Dearest Annie,

At last night's class BB spent a lot of time on a poem of Brownstein's (the plump dark young guy, whom I rather like), using some of its positive things and negative things to make general points about style, writing phrases, using manners of speaking, etc. But the result was diffuse, so I haven't much to tell you except for a few isolated comments:

Through the history of literature, oddly enough, satirists have been considered the best stylists. They're more calculating, consider and weigh each word, their intention is faster, shrewder. Examples: Swift, Rabelais, Cervantes, Shakespeare (esp. comedies), Joyce, Pound (esp. in short epigrammatic poems), Chaucer when funny. Contrast with Dostoyevsky—powerful and moving, but not always marvelous in choice of words.

More lyrical and personal poetry carries reader or hearer along by means of sentiments and good-will, but also carries along with it a great deal more dross. Written in *phrases* rather than single words. Take Ginsberg—goes on and on with feelings building up energy through feelings and convictions and rhythms—it's all his autobiography and there's a near-mythic element in that—wants to proclaim his own exaltation in his life, his body, his sex, etc. Is concerned with being on a large scale—heaven, time, eternity, love. A religious poet telling us to stop war, stop being ashamed of sex, stop nonsense about money, stop hemming and hawing, stop being boring, etc. (Note from me: I agree, but I do wish AG were not so repulsive—I heard his reading with his father taped and broadcast on RVR and I just cannot share his glory in his own shit—can you?)

WC Williams and Ginsberg have something in common and of course AG was encouraged and influenced by WCW and both are in Whitman tradition. In an essay Williams stated "The poem is a field of action." Believed in people, love, etc. Listened to common speech and used it constantly. Their poems meant to be read aloud. Speech (phrases) always in top of their minds. Williams not always perfect word by word, Ginsberg's words not always pleasing or best choices—aim at total overall effect, rolling sentences, long paragraphs. (Note from me: Have never liked Whitman and have reservations about Ginsberg's poems—am not speaking here of his personal style—but like some of his shorter things, find them sharp and successful. BUT I like Williams very much indeed for his civilized wisdom and perceptions—irony, compassion, not so concerned with his self as the other two, not bombastic as they are. Not homosexual, either, which I'm sure gives him a less limited view of life. Also there's more sensitiveness and real beauty in his writing.)

Williams produced more than any other poet writing in this century in English. He and Edmund Wilson were the first and almost the only known writers (critics) to "get" *FINNEGANS WAKE* when it first came out (in sections) in *Transition*. (Eugene Jolas's magazine in Paris, I believe.) Everybody else thought Joyce had gone off his rocker.

Pound had reservations, Eliot detached himself from it completely.

BB read a bit from Mayakovsky, who has similarities with WCW and AG, talked a bit about his legend (was considered official poet of Russian revolution but got disappointed with Soviet Union under Stalin—loved a White Russian woman in Paris—couldn't be with her and she couldn't go back to SU—suicide about 1930)—translations of Mayakovsky lose puns, turns of Russian phrases, etc. Other reading: some Ginsberg, a part of Wms. PATERSON. Mentioned Poe as concerned with pure sound, some of the Dadaists concerned with pure sound but also with typographical effects—breaking up words on page and all that—trying to "free" the word.

All this sort of thing poses overall questions for me, especially when I hear other people, like some of the poets reading on RVR, also talk about "freeing" the word, or quoting McLuhan as saying "words are on the way out." If you think this through what does it really mean? Free the word for *what*? Joyce, now, was trying to free words from stale associations to make them richer and open up treasures for us. And the semanticists, who flourished during the 1930s, were trying to make everybody use words more carefully, precisely, with scientific exactitude and explicitness, so that we could communicate with each other better and not be emotional in our use of speech and solve our political problems. You can see that they have a point. But what's ahead for the WORD? Occasionally I read that some scientific visionary says that by the year 2000 knowledge will be injected into our nervous systems directly from computer storages by means of electrodes—UGH!

BB said he'd seen Stephanie Gordon and Kenneth Noland last weekend and SG told him it's possible to go to B'ington by plane so maybe, etc. But I suspect he procrastinates too much and probably won't make it.

Lewis had told me he'd like to visit the class last night and would meet me and go, but he didn't show up. I waited downstairs till the last minute.

Carl telephoned Sunday evening. No special news, just has a lot of work ahead.

Nina's name day (St. Irene) is tomorrow and she invited us to come up after dinner for cake, coffee, wine, etc. She's also invited Marie Farnsworth, Yeffe Kimball and husband Harvey Slatin, Andrew and Ruth, and others. I must get her a present. We went to Klein's and Gimbels last Saturday and she tried on a lot of things but didn't buy anything except some pure white jeans (very chic) and some stockings. She was glad to know about those stores though. She was in a sort of depressed state, over Angelo and all that, and didn't feel very glamorous. I was hoping she'd find something sensational that would cheer her up but it wasn't our day for that.

So long for now, with kisses,
Mummy

Called Cyril and he finally sent me the reading schedule for May. See they got Cohen at last—he's lucky to be on with Levertov. H. Weiner & Barbara Myers are from BB class—C. said he's mailed you one too.

Friday, 6 May 1966

Dearest Annie,

Nice weather, lots of events here. This is always the time of year when there's a lot to do, it seems. People go about more because it's not so cold, do more inviting before the summer vacations start, there are more little plays and modern concerts, and so on.

We were at Nina's last night. Another Greek Irene shared the celebration with her so there were various Greek friends of both and lots and lots of food, retsina, etc. Our Nina told me quietly that her parents had telephoned her yesterday morning, and at one point her father said, How is HE? and she said, Who? and he said, Angelo, of course, so she just said Oh, he's fine. But they probably will be beginning to catch on to the fact that things haven't worked out. She feels almost as sad about their disappointment as her own. A. has not called her or anything though he sometimes asks mutual friends (who were there last night) how she's doing. The friends had said (probably having urged him) that he might drop by the party late, but he hadn't by the time I left. Daddy stuck the evening out pretty valiantly—I don't think it was too hard on him as he had a few attractive young girls to talk to—but when he was ready to leave Marie Farnsworth wanted to stay longer and have me to ride downtown with so I stayed too. Andrew and Ruth were there, A. in fine form (has a big moustache now), R. a little too matronly and motherly now for people's taste—Daddy says she's lost her glamor—she talks about the baby to everyone, etc. You'll have to do something about Andrew—he is determined to have you up to their place for dinner. Do you remember once finding some Karayosi (Greek paper cut-out-puppets) on 8th St. or near soon after you came home? They've been lying around and I saw that one of the sheets had Alexander the Great, so took it to give Andrew for the baby. It was quite a sensation—all the Greeks were overjoyed and wanted to know where I'd got it, so I said you'd found it. A. probably thinks you got it recently on purpose for his baby so I'm telling you in case it ever comes up. I found plenty of Greeks to talk to—one man from the U.N. who knew a lot about Sikelianos, another whose family was from a village very near Sykia, so he knew the place and a lot of the people there and even remembered hearing about *me*, a very nice young Greek-American girl who's never been to Greece because her father left for political reasons and is afraid to let her go there—she's studying opera singing and has a role in a summer company in Colorado; we talked a lot about music—I guess I was the only person there who was interested in anything about her career.

Wednesday evening Jean Howard and I went to a contemporary concert at the NYU Loeb (Composers' Showcase) and it turned out I was sitting right behind Elliott Carter! I was as thrilled as a schoolgirl about a movie star. I recognized him at intermission (I'd seen him before) then when his beautiful, beautiful cello sonata was played in the second half (superbly by Bernard Greenhouse) he got up for his bow so I was sure. Of course Jean and I, walking right next to him in the aisle at the end, spoke to him and of course he was charming. He said what a pity we have so many marvelous musicians for contemporary works and so few audiences, which is the ghastly truth. The Loeb was like $^2/_3$ full but quite a few left at intermission.

Forgot to say what I took Nina: a gay printed cotton head cover-up, the sort that ties at the back (to wear in Israel in the sun) and a pair of white fishnets. She seemed pleased.

Yesterday Kay Edgar invited me to lunch with two other women at her place and then on to a tour of houses in the Village for the benefit of the Friendly Visitors (Protestant women who try to help inmates at the Womens House of Detention, take them magazines, clothing, etc.). All the places were on Ninth or Tenth St. west of Fifth except the last at Waverly & 6th and that turned out to be Mary Bancroft Boulton's, the same one described in the Times clipping I sent you. Mary wasn't there when we were, we just missed her. Funny thing: Gretchen Manton, who was one of us, just called me to say that she and Jimmy went to a dinner at the University Club last night and Mr. and Mrs. Boulton happened to be at their table and how charming they were. Pretty funny combination, I'd say. Well, it might be fine if the Mantons got to know more people like that—it might help them lose some of their archaic prejudices.

The house I liked was Helena Simkhovitch Didisheim's—she's a sculptor and daughter of Greenwich House founders. Everything in simple and excellent taste—I know it would be your choice too. I'd seen it before. These tours are fun and very revealing about people. Naturally I've my own private opinions as I go along—psychological, sociological, aesthetic and intellectual judgments all rolled together. One of the flossiest places had a SleepMate by the master's bed—Daddy's IN!

Nina said she ran into Mark the other day on 5th Ave, and they decided to meet and have lunch together today at the Modern Museum.

Carl wrote that he doesn't expect to get down or even away from Hamilton before the end of term, which is only three weeks away now—too much work, study for exams, and so on. I guess we'll send him a check to spend, if he can find anything to do or buy up there, on his birthday. Sending books that he'd have to bring home, or clothing, or other objects, would be sort of senseless, and his record player is down here for repairs now, a roommate broke the arm (and will pay).

Tonight we're both going to a staged reading of a new play by Lionel Abel about Kierkegaard at the Theatre for Ideas (Broughton) and tomorrow night to hear the GREAT MCLUHAN. This clipping from this week's VOICE about a conference of linguists and Eng. high school teachers last week gives a fairly good idea of what we can expect. If there's anything new said I'll report it to you, though.

Quote from Edmund Wilson in an article on him by Frank Kermode in newest *Encounter*: "All activity, in whatever field it takes place, is an attempt to give meaning to our experience—that is, to make life more practicable." (This is as true of the fictions of Sophocles as of Euclid, says Kermode.) "Art has its origin in the need to pretend that human life is something other than it is, and, in a sense, by pretending this, it succeeds to some extent in transforming it.". . . Also Kermode goes on, "The transformation of the world, as Wallace Stevens remarked, is the transformation of ourselves, and we do it with reason and imagination." . . . Just thought these notions might possibly be applicable to Roethke.

Love & kisses,
Mummy

Sunday, 8 May 1966

Dearest A.,

McLuhan looks like a professor stereotype: tweedy, lanky, craggy, Fiftyish, brown-haired, talks fast, obviously would rather make a wise crack than give a straight answer or utter a straight statement. YMHA overflowing, standees, people seated on both sides of stage. No introduction—he came right out and plunged in with same opening remarks about DEWline greetings (Distant Early Warning) as in 2 speeches at NYU quoted in VOICE piece, thereby confirming a prediction Daddy had made to me that he would begin that way here also. Following gems are what I managed to note down on my program or remember for your delectation:

Cool—his use of this word has gotten him into lots of hot water (laughter) but it applies to the style of this age and it means *both involved and detached*, Eliot's 4 Quartets a perfect illustration.

Have we noticed how children always use *cool* and all other current slang correctly? They *know*, because their perceptiveness is not yet dulled.

A cat chased a mouse under the floorboards. Mouse waited, then heard an ar-rk ar-rk and bow-wow, thought Ah, the dog has chased the cat and I can go out and he did. The cat pounced on him and as he did so and started to chew him said, "You see it's an advantage to be bi-lingual."

Modern man is moving out of the world of the specialist (19th century's product) with resulting fragmentation, alienation, categorization, into the world of the *hunter*, when the only real work (aside from essentials to maintain life, etc.) will be *discovery, knowing*.

Paleolithic Man, the hunter, became planter, cultivator, will become hunter again.

Identity lost in *jobs*—future work will restore identity in *roles*.

Men will look forward to old age as period of more knowing & discovery.

The 20th century child is the hardest-working child there has ever been because of all the information he must assimilate thanks to electronics.

The *retrieval* (of information) system of computers is just about the greatest result of electronics. The instant shuffling through layers and layers and layers of information opens up an infinity of new combinations, associations.

In language it is the pun that retrieves information from different levels of meaning all at once and suggests new meanings. *Finnegans Wake* (of course!). Joyce saw Language as the richest treasure in existence which would yield up all rewards if explored.

As soon as anything is transferred to a new environment it becomes a work of art because it is looked at with fresh perceptions.

We are making our planet into a work of art.

The space capsule is the first man-made environment—but you have to take it with you.

XEROX is revolutionizing the publishing industry—in the future writers will xerox their books for distribution themselves—teachers will write and xerox textbooks for classes. Books in the future will be just information services, tailor-made and custom-built—few will read for any other purpose but info.

A newspaper is a *happening*—all those absolutely disparate stories presented side by side, only thing that connects them is dateline. Without that they'd be pure surrealist poems.

Our environment is an all-at-once image for each of us.

The problems of the past were *conceptual*. Now they are *perceptual*.

Teaching is still largely conceptual, looking to past. We are now moving forward so fast (technologically, instant communication, out into space, and all that) that we'll have to learn to look at what's under our noses rather than in the rear mirror. Standard teaching method has always been considered "proceeding from the known to the unknown." This no good now. We must look forward into the unknown, and then, if we must, translate it into the known for present uses.

The amounts of information on all levels that are now available outside schools greatly exceed those in classrooms. Never like this before—classroom was the only place to learn. Information is inventories of *effects*. The medium plus the environment gives the process.

(Speaking of the medium, forgot to say that right at beginning of lecture he said cutely "The medium is the *massage*—(laughter)—it massages and massages everybody all the time.")

In the 18th century the artist (and poet) looked at the world as if it were a landscape to be framed, and painted or wrote about it as if it were in a frame, thereby having profound effect on mentality of people of the age—it was something they looked *out* on, & classified.

(Contrast mediaeval art—a celebration, festive, close to life. Or Balinese art. In Bali *everything* is done with grace and beauty, even the way the people move. Consequently the Balinese say, "We have no art, we simply do everything as well as possible.")

Pop art, now, is a means of perception and participation, not classification.

In the middle of the 19th century, mainly because of Baudelaire, Rimbaud, Mallarmé, there was a change over into a concern with the inner life. The meaning of a work of art became to probe within the self, Flaubert: "Style is a way of knowing, of seeing." Symbolism, exploring the inner lands. And on to Joyce, surrealism, etc.

Today our awareness has been extended through electronics till it embraces the total human environment. Now the function of art is to teach *perception*, make us see.

If you could examine the total present closely enough you would be able to anticipate all possible futures.

In 1880 Seurat painted like TV, dots with light as if projected from behind painting.

A cartoon demands more participation from the observer than a photograph does. (De Gaulle at an art exhibit said, "Who's that a cartoon of over there?". . . . "But, monsieur, that is a mirror!" Laughter.)

Advertising demands no involvement but spells out what the effect will be of owning the product. More people now read the advts. *after* buying the product than before, to find out what they have. Or the advt. simply becomes a substitute for the product and they don't buy.

The West is becoming orientalized at the same time the East is becoming more westernized. (He was asked later to illustrate this, said (1) the growth of inwardness—example of Thomas Merton moving from monastery to becoming a real hermit, (2) our children take themselves more seriously, look for "involvement", are role-oriented rather than job-oriented, and (3) take dancing (social)—in the day of the foxtrot (his own day) you had a big floor to move around on sweepingly, now you and your partner stay on a few square inches of floor and create images.)

TV has destroyed the story line in movies and novels. No narratives any more, just modulations of the complex environment. Fellini as example. IN COLD BLOOD in 18th century would have been a straight narrative. Now it's an environmental shake-up.

School and college drop-outs drop out often because they cannot make contact with the environment.

He McLuhan (and I thought this was interesting) began his studies out of *irritation* at the modern world the way it's going—he's only a simple teacher of literature and he sees literacy disappearing. But the more he got into it the more fascinated he grew because he might just as well. Every so often in the course of the lecture he would say, "Now I'm not saying this is either good or bad, desirable or not—I'm not making *any* moral judgments."

Along with the story line have disappeared the hemline, the waistline, and the stagline. (*Much* laughter.)

★★★

It was a very intelligent looking audience, well-dressed, no rock-and-roll types or Village beats at all. The longest hair I saw, and that's not very long, was on Bill Berkson, who was sitting several rows in front of us. Had a feeling he'd be there. He noticed me first, turned around and waved gaily. Must have had a lot of friends in audience, saw him waving a lot at end. Probably lots of art world there, saw Betty Parsons for one. BB was with several other people, including a dame who came to class with him once, probably girlfriend of moment—odd-looking—small, neat, chic, but has a strange face that looks old from a distance (while he looks boyish)—I had wondered if she was his mother before

I saw her close! Her eyes are oddly set, lifeless and maybe lashless or something, very detached expressionless look . . . Cool. Marian Tracy was with us and we met Dick Gill, Daddy's colleague, and went for coffee afterward. (Dick is nice—maybe you remember his coming up to Stratford to Kim's with us, so long ago.)

I've just read a book I found very exciting—THE (DIBLOS) NOTEBOOK, Merrill not just because the setting is a Greek one and very familiar to me—a made-up island near Paros, where I lived and Troezen (home of Phaedra), but more because of the technique. As the title says, it's a notebook, and it's about a novel with false starts, crossed-out words and phrases, ideas jotted down, interpolated comments and self-criticisms, and a little straight writing, all put together quite poetically. Merrill is a poet and also wrote "The Bait" in that book of short plays you have (by Ashbery and O'Hara and Abel, with his.) Greek characters and characteristics all skillfully shown, impressions of both village and intellectual scenes, etc.

I thought the spring weather had come for good but it's coldish again and nasty and wet today.

David Grimm called yesterday, back from Europe, to say hello and ask about you. He had of course a wonderful time till his money was spent, so came back to make more to go back when he can. Is auditioning. Tried out for some Great Lakes Shakespeare. Thinks Ashley-Famous will take him as a client; which may help. He sent you his best.

Daddy got your letter yesterday and seemed pleased to be written to.

You may have overlooked this item in the art column and I'm sure it'll interest you.

Love & kisses,
Mummy

Monday, 9 May 1966

Dearest Annie,

Hope you won't mind my opening this "rejection slip" from the London Academy. I thought they'd write you at Bennington before this, so have been assuming it was unfavorable or you'd have let us know, especially since you'd told me just how few places they offer. I'm disappointed for you, of course—it would be silly to pretend not to be, but it needn't be a traumatic experience. You're pretty sturdy, and I'm sure you haven't counted on getting in. Maybe it's best to be fatalistic about setbacks and say, well, destiny must be saving you for a better opportunity or at least keeping you from something that would not have been right! I use this device myself and it's a good one because maybe it's true. Anyway, I know you can be a fine actress and there are plenty of other places to study.

                              Love & kisses,
                              Mummy

Thursday, 12 May 1966

Dearest Annie,

Poets read Tuesday night were *Yeats*: "Major Robert Gregory" (turning point in development of Y's rhetoric) from WILD SWANS AT COOLE, "Byzantium", and "Sailing to Byzantium"; *Williams*: more from PATERSON, "The Yachts", and "Poem for Norman McLeod"; and *David Schubert* (1913-1946—ever hear of him?): "The Happy Traveler", "Detroit Free Press", and "The Simple Scale."

Comments: By late 19th century English literary language was relatively set and dead compared with American—all those fresh idioms. It was said the Victorians tried to *speak* like Eng. written prose, but which came first? The prose was already Victorian—life and language intermix, Irish language on the other hand was unburdened by literature—offered imagination, inflection, energy. Remember, though, BB stressed how it was dying and Joyce revived it—maybe he meant basic English, not just Irish.

Yeats had an aristocratic voice in an anti-aristocratic context—speaks to reader directly but with an oratorical flair—his speech is weighted with rhetoric but balloons upward. His life was actually not very eventful—social contacts were all cozy drawing room type—even his great passion for Maude Gonne was on a lofty level—nothing pornographic about him. His late poems though marvelous are an old man's poems—not always inspiring to young. Both Auden and MacNeice specially influenced by "Phoenix."

Pound was a "pure literacy gentleman"—put scarcely anything personal into his poems—they reveal nothing much about his life.

Williams has wide appeal because democratic. In beginning scholars & critics thought him too "homey"—not cultivated enough (actually he knew more Greek than Pound—had tremendous background, widely read himself). But he didn't flaunt erudition in poems as Eliot did, also Pound (justifiably because to him poetry and language *were* treasures of erudition), also Marianne Moore. Williams has influenced many many poets by now—Duncan (who's also influenced by Eliot), Lowell (at his best, which a lot of the time he isn't—BB finds a lot of contrived symbolism and bombast there) and others.

BB does not think *Zukofsky* a good poet.

Thinks Charles *Olson* worth reading for music of poetry—a good teacher—his poetics ("Projective Verse") make sense.

David Schubert, born Brooklyn, educated Amherst and I think City, was one of the few poets in a tragic generation (tragic because killed in War II before they could even develop their talent) who managed to write some marvelous things that were not corrupted by the criticism of the period. Both O'Hara and Koch influenced by him. His only book published was a small paperback by Macmillan—INITIAL A. I'll try to get it but don't know if I can. (I don't think *he* was killed in the war, died of illness, but he was of that period—died at only 33.) Maybe in B'ington library?

On criticism: The "close reading" attack, which takes the poem as a thing to be torn apart like a mechanical clock to see what makes it work, tracking down each symbol, Freudian myth, literary allusion, classical reference, etc., had distorting destructive effect on beginning poets of the period 1920 through 1940s. A lot of it goes on still, especially in college courses and graduate schools. Poets *liked* to be treated this way because it sold a lot of their books—sold critics' books too—the exegesis was more important than the poetry. Leading critics of this school: I.A. Richards, Cleanth Brooks, Robert Penn Warren, R.P. Blackmur. They took poets away from the main business of poetry, which is language— result, no *greatness*. (Suppose this last statement could be debated, for who knows?)

Schejldahl asked about *Ashbery*—how much is he influenced by Eliot? because he has been noticing similarities between "The Skaters" and the "FOUR QUARTETS." BB agreed there are many points of resemblance—highly civilized tone—the give-and-take of irony back and forth (though this comes from real moods and is not mincing)— exquisite filigrees of irony—interest in metaphysical questions—what is real and eternal? what is not real?—Ashbery for all his "French pretensions" is an Anglican type.

Well, we have two more classes with BB. Not many of us are left.

Hannah Weiner hasn't come since BB criticized her preoccupation with "color"—maybe a coincidence, maybe she couldn't take it. Evidently Schejldahl is working for a degree and taking courses for credit—he mentioned another course and some finals. BB said that at the last session he's going to try to make each of us see that we have fixed notions about ourselves in relation to our writing and get us to admit it even if he has to give us LSD—big joke? Is this news? Could I step outside of Frances W.—or outside of being a woman—long enough to write something completely objective, if that's what he's driving at? I do pretty well at splitting myself up as it is, I think. Well, it sounds interesting. But he'll probably forget what he said and not bring the confession idea up at all unless I remind him. I might. I got him to talk about McLuhan a bit. Some of the class didn't know a thing, so he gave a summary of the approach. Did you know McL. is a "hot" Roman Catholic? BB said John Cage told *him* they had lunch last Friday and McL. said he's not "ecumenical"—still wants his fish Fridays. BB said: McL. is not a genius but he starts people thinking, breaks up some of their set notions; one of the most interesting things about THE GUTENBERG GALAXY is the bibliography, a provocative one; the people in the McL. "cult" are not to be taken seriously but McL. himself has a very interesting critical coterie: Hugh Kenner, Father Ong, (S.J.), Buckminster Fuller, some people in cybernetics, et al. BB said read current issue of "The American Scholar" with articles by McL. and others. I got it on the way home and it's full of meat. The McL. piece (a speech he gave at a conference last fall on the future, etc.) is practically the same speech we heard, plus more things we didn't hear. It even has the same beginning and the same jokes. Evidently McL. is carrying out his own doctrine and thinks the speech itself is the speech, ha! I know that mag. is in your library so you can have a look at it.

The latest *Voice* has a 3-page article absolutely tearing McL. to bits, not for his talk, the writer couldn't get in, but for his shoddy scholarship, misstatements, etc. in books. They must think he's *dangerous* to democracy or something.

We're going uptown to dinner tonight at the Sampsons'—those lovely academic people from Colorado U. I told you about—friends of Marie Farnsworth. Think I'll go hear RD Cohen read tomorrow evening.

Love & kisses,
Mummy

Friday, 13 May 1966

Dearest Annie,

Like your poem very much. Whole effect is both strong and "delicate"—progression of images builds up nicely.

Enclosing two of my own. I dashed off "Philadelphia" very quickly before class the other night because I had only one other ready to turn in. Of course it's slight and superficial, as most of my things are. On the other hand, when I have written about states of mind that have been important to me my readers—few as they are—haven't seemed to consider the results successful, with one or two exceptions. A ticklish business, but that's part of the fun and challenge. I really don't care at all about SILO's not using the Aeschylus adaptation (it's not really a translation) though privately I think your committee's awfully "backward." Perhaps I should care more about publication, or about trying to be published, but when I look through all the anthologies and cast a jaundiced eye over the dusty pile of little magazines at Eli's and read some of the critics of the recent past and listen to some of the drivel on radio readings I *know* that there's no precise correspondence between quality and recognition at all, even though it's a nice warm comfortable feeling to have somebody—even just one person—really "get" what you mean. In all the millions of words of poetry written in English alone since the first bards started having somebody record theirs so few lines have been memorable. Most of them are in Shakespeare, still. This doesn't depress me—on the contrary I find it truly exciting that any at all really make it up to some special height. To me this is very significant—an indication of absolute value somewhere in our human experience, the proof offered by qualitative difference between the merely good and the "wonderful."

Forgive me for stealing a bit of your own experience and information from Philadelphia but I'm sure you'd write a very different version and a much better one. I've used some of my own knowledge of the structure and setting, from travelling through and visiting some of the upper class people a long time ago. It's not meant to be anything but a little impressionistic collage, but a stereotyped moral judgment slipped in in spite of my usually trying to avoid making any.

What is a "gig"—jazz term, I suppose, but I don't know it.

Yesterday I got an anonymous letter saying why don't I wash my filthy windows, they are a disgrace like the ones of the rooming house next door to me and I ought to be ashamed of myself because spring is here. I suppose it was sent by some old woman in the tenement across the street. I think it's funny, though I shan't tell Daddy because he might get paranoiac. Actually, she (or he, though I doubt it's a he) is right—they are filthy and a disgrace and I have been planning to call a window washer one of these days but procrastinate and then it's rained so much. My correspondent was wrong about the weather, at least— after two beautiful days it's been cold and rainy again like last week. Lee Roberts and I have ordered wrought iron gates for our famous stoops. They'll take about 2 weeks and after that I'll try to do a little brightening up. They won't have locks, but self-closing hinges. We don't expect them to solve our problems completely, but they will be something of a deterrent. The hoods who stroll by at night won't be quite so likely to stop and loiter if they have to open a gate to get on the steps and be penned in while they sit—I *hope!* We'd better be prepared psychologically for some more egg-throwing, though, or other possible retaliation before they get over the initial shock and get used to its existence. It's costing $120 each but I think it'll be worth a lot more if it helps ease the situation at all.

Daddy and I had a nice evening with the Sampsons. Ed S. is a professor of engineering at Colorado, but his hobby is Shakespeare. They're warm, gentle, outgoing, extremely intelligent. I wish they weren't going back—this has been a sabbatical year. They've just bought a 36-foot yacht (with aux. motor) and plan to spend the summer around New England Coast and Canada, with their three younger children. Their oldest is the girl I told you about who got married in the fall and had a baby at Christmas and is finishing her senior year at Col. with her husband. Their youngest is a 9-year girl who sat around with us—just a marvelous, lovely child. Daddy seemed quite enchanted by her. He and I have almost—though not quite—forgotten just how wonderful it was to have a little girl that age around. John's right, it's a very special sort of charm—there's nothing else quite like it. The other 2 Sampson kids, a 14-yr. boy at E.I. and a 16-yr. girl at the U.N. school, were busy with homework in their rooms. The family rooming arrangement is a preposterous one for these times but they are hilarious about it and it seems to have gone all right. Lisa, the youngest, shares her parents' room and the other two room together—there are only 2 bedrooms. This in a penthouse on the upper east side! A city welfare worker would surely be shocked and try to do something about this.

I'm sure the reason you couldn't get though to Carl by phone Sunday was all the Mothers Day jamming by the unenlightened—the *Times* even had a little item about it. Nice for business!

Love and kisses,
Mummy

[undated, probably mid–May 1966]

Saturday morning

Dear Annie,

Yesterday afternoon I was on 8th St, and stopped in Bookshop to look around and congratulate Ted Wilentz on his recent election as president of Nat'l Booksellers of America and tell his brother Eli about seeing Johnny Ginnes (we used to see him & family at the G.'s birthdays) and I also took a look at how your publications are selling (present stock: SILO 8 (1), SILO 9 (10), ANGEL HAIR (5)) and I also looked for the Jespersen book B. Berkson showed us and it's called ESSENTIALS OF ENGLISH GRAMMAR, 2.95 and is a regular though superior handbook and near the poetry magazine section I noticed this book by Andrea Dworkin high up on the wall so I got it in case you haven't seen it though I'm aware it may have been around Bennington. I was curious about it myself. She has a command of poetic language but what depressing and tedious content, especially in her long prose poem, which is like some dreadful smelly too-copious menstrual flux, bad Ginsberg-cum-Genêt. I wonder what Francis Golffing, to whom it's dedicated, will think of it. Which reminds me that I never got to meet or see him and I still don't know what he looks like though Daddy seems to remember your pointing him out; I must have been looking the other way.

I'm using Carl's Olympia because the carriage lever on my Olivetti is broken and I must take it uptown. This is a nice machine, just like yours, I guess.

The next time you come over will you bring your Hart Crane paper for me to read? Also several more copies of ANGEL HAIR and SILO 9—if you haven't stamped them all with Perreault's name bring me unstamped ones because it does spoil the appearance, although I suppose it was a good idea to stamp it for around here where he may see it and would object to being left off, though I'm sure more people would notice his name inside than outside anyway.

Carl sent us a brass rubbing from Oxford, of a medieval lady praying, very nice—he made it himself.

Love,
Frances

Steve Wolff called to congratulate you on graduation, etc. he was in town from New Haven just briefly. This poem is in a volume of his which Daddy must return to Pace—I like it and thought you might also, particularly because of Burke and the response to his rhetoric.

Monday, May 16 1966

Dearest Annie,

Here's the poem you asked for. I'll be interested in seeing your version if you do one. Also enclose another I wrote yesterday.

Tried calling Carl for 1½ hours last night but couldn't get through and gave up at midnight. It wasn't urgent, but we'd agreed I would. Maybe I'll try tonight, or he'll call.

Hope you've sent him a copy of ANGEL HAIR. Ours arrived today and I read it through. It's certainly good-looking. Your poem is definitely one of the best—has a real strength that's lacking in others—unusual for a girl to have that particular vitality. (By the way, have you seen Sandra Hochman's new book? I have it from the library and it's pretty bad—dismally inferior to her MANHATTAN PASTURES, in which I rather liked some poems—they had a pleasing bright charm. Too bad.)

Think I'll buy a copy on 8ᵗʰ St. and give it to Berkson. I certainly would like to send it around to other people—Dona, Millicent, the Sampsons, others you don't know, but old Jon's stupid bits of pornography make it difficult. It would just embarrass <u>them</u>. Well, maybe another issue will be available. Too bad about Levertov's misspelling. Next time if you've doubts check with the author.

Since you're in the magazine business you may find this piece on *The Harvard Advocate* interesting.

I think I've told you vaguely that I've been putting some money away slowly for the last several years so I'd have something to help you study further when you finished Bennington, or get started in the theatre. That's what I'd have used if you'd gotten into the Academy. Well, no use worrying about that, but do be thinking of possible alternatives. I can't help feeling that your education has really just begun and shouldn't be cut short now. I've enough to send you abroad, if you can find a project. Another consideration: do you really think you ought to take David's advice about Papp's company as final, without talking to other people, Tom S. for instance? What does David know about it from the point of view of an actor, anyway? His situation is different, though I've no doubt he hears a lot of scuttlebutt. Still, having been in a Papp play is a reasonable credit, and as you know he's going to be building up a year-round company in his new theatre in the old Astor Place building. Don't overlook *any* possibilities—you really can't afford to until you've built up a whole array of them to choose from—though I don't mean you should take anything really crappy. But I don't think Papp's company is that bad—it still has some standing—more than Lincoln Center right now, it appears. APA is the only *good* name in town this year! I'm also prepared to finance you if you want to study something incidental like French—as you know it's one of my insistent desires, to have you able to chatter fluently in your lovely voice.

Just got the low-down from Lee Roberts on the drug raid Friday evening. As it happened, Frances was having a teenage party at the time—her whole class from school—all nice, well-behaved kids. Lee had one hell of a time persuading the police that it was the top floor they wanted to search, and then nothing was found. Hal thinks the dame had been tipped off. The warrant was actually made out for the older daughter's boyfriend.

Love and kisses,
Mummy

Tuesday, May 17 1966

Dearest Annie,

BB telephoned and cancelled tonight's class, I don't know why because I was out and Joanie took message. He did say we'll meet next week. Suppose that'll be the last session. I was disappointed tonight and there was nothing else I wanted to do, so watched Murray the K's latest show, it's one way to keep up with *your* brave new world. The theme was supposedly the "year 2000" but they certainly didn't get very far into the future—in fact Daddy pointed out to me numerous instances of really "old-hat" things. As far as the music goes nothing was new except arrangements and the electronic amplification. The performers were all pretty good—THE ANIMALS, Joe Tex and his group, *et al.* M. the K rather overworked the phrase "frame of reference" in trying to bridge the gap between the "generations." Actually he himself is an aging parent—all of 40, with kids. The great philosophy of the young, he said, and they all said, right on cue, is "honesty." You do what you like and nobody should blame you for it because you're being "honest." Ha. Well, I try to be honest too, but I *start* there and try to use a lot of feedback to test myself. Ho hum, plus ça change. . . .

In the middle of the show on came Holland in her mouth wash commercial and actually she wasn't bad at all. She had a nice smile and a very distinct flair, is a real pro. I called her up and told her so and she was pleased because the material of the commercials is so depressing and she hasn't gotten anything else but commercials yet, though she's been to some auditions. She has a lot of difficulty finding good scenes to use in auditions, she said. She was up at Bennington last weekend but felt very tired and didn't go around—stayed in and played cards. Nina is rehearsing in the Open Theatre for something to be done at the Café Cino. I guess when one's in a spot like Holland's one has to take the line of just trying to do whatever is available as well as possible. Kim probably has made up her mind to that too, for she's been in a lot of soap operas and such lately. She was in Dr. Kildare tonight— Daddy caught part of it—playing a mother whose daughter is hurt in an accident and the doctors at the hospital discover she's pregnant—a real tear-jerker.

Well, we now have a gate across our famous stoop. The men came and put it up this morning and I had a great time hanging around with the boss (a character) and listening to the comments by kids when they came out of school and saw the men working: "Hey, lady, whatcha put that up for, how we gonna play ball?" "Hey, miss, howya gonna get inya house?" "Hey, that's the place we play ball, why ya put that fence up?" After school several of them tried playing for a while but I don't think the game was too successful. The gate goes across the second step (we couldn't put it on the bottom one because the property line doesn't extend quite that far and Lee didn't want the city telling us we had a violation) and the ball doesn't bounce up at the right angle when they have to throw it so low down. Of course they may be ingenious enough to develop a new game. But it won't be the same, and it certainly isn't handy for sitting now. The gate does not lock, but it is self-closing. We'll see what happens. Daddy is pleased and so are the Robertses. The only resident who doesn't like it is Joanie—she said it looks UNFRIENDLY. Just what we want, I told her, but it isn't directed at her and *she* used to throw water on the boys herself.

Spoke with Carl last night and he didn't sound too depressed but he said Saturday was a pretty grim day all around. He's shelved his anxiety for the moment, anyway, so I've put mine aside too. Which, alas, is not the same thing as getting rid of it because things turn out all right. Carl had received ANGEL HAIR and thought it was "nice." I don't think he'd read all of it. He's been enjoying his music course, he said—they are doing the impressionists—Ravel, Debussy—and the post-impressionists and into the moderns. Even some electronic music—Stockhausen. And of course Bartok. He asked if we have the record of the Music for Strings, Percussion, etc. as he liked it.

Tomorrow night I'm going to Totty West Sullivan's dance concert at the Judson. She and another girl have done the choreography and she will dance also. I'd have planned to go tonight, the first performance of two, if I'd known about the class being cancelled. Had already made plans and reservations for tomorrow for Marian Tracy and self. Connie and Bob are nervous as all get-out about whether it will come off—*all* parents are sensitive to their children and want things to go well that they do. Like me, I felt proud today when I bought a couple of ANGEL HAIRs at the 8th St. and the clerk said, "This is very nice." He wasn't one of your special pals, either, for he didn't know your name. There were about 7 copies there, up in the back. Was going to take BB one, will do next week.

Love & kisses,
Mummy

Sunday, 29 May 1966

Darling Annie,

That's a very nice poem you sent. Am I right in feeling it's connected with some of your states of mind about finishing college?

It's funny, though not surprising, how your letter is practically an answer to mine written at the same time. I know you hate "dialogues" on emotional questions and I'll try to keep this from being any "lengthy reply" since you asked me not to write one. But I must clear up a few points or have them cleared up for me:

1) Your statement, "I know nothing I ever do will satisfy you completely," is just not true. Period. I look forward to a long series of pleasant occasions for great satisfaction and pride.

2) I don't "get" what you "mean" when you write . . . "often I feel your demands on me are physical, that is, the most difficult for me." Are you referring to Daddy's and my enjoyment of your physical presence? For we do enjoy it despite all the troubles between us. We love to look at you, talk with you, and hear about what you're doing, and your beauty, wit and charm have always been one of the pure delights of our lives; I'm not exaggerating . . . Or do you mean what you evidently feel are efforts on my part to interfere with your sex life? This, of course, is the major issue and actually the *only* cause of our difficulties. Will you, please, please, sweet, lovely baby, try once for all, with an open mind, to understand my attitude: AMBIVALENT, confused, frightened, anxious, but *loving*. I love sex myself and am very sympathetic to your needs and drives. I'm glad you are not frigid, I'm glad you've found a compatible partner, or partners, I *know* how important this is, and furthermore I do

understand that the environment in which you've grown up has unusual pressures and I think you've handled yourself with more intelligence than many other girls . . . At the same time, if I hadn't tried to hold you back to some extent from getting too involved too young I wouldn't have been able to face myself with a clear conscience. From now on, of course, the responsibility for shaping your life is your own. As Mike Allen said, I simply have to learn to face the possibility that you may make tragic mistakes. But as long as I live I'll be available for anything you may want or need from me. So will Daddy.

3)   I am painfully aware of a great deal of ugliness in the environment and I am perhaps over-sensitive about your reputation. But can't you accept this about me and avoid being too flagrant? It just isn't true (as yet) that everybody thinks sexual freedom is OK—and perhaps it isn't, either. Perhaps I am so sensitive because I've been called a "whore" and heard that it was being said of me that "Glaukos's wife *is rotting*"—a single word in Greek and much more powerful than the English. The fact is that I felt it was *true*, and it was enough to make me break off that affair for good, thank goodness. I had to go through it, but I'm sorry it was necessary.

4)   Are you quite aware that Daddy has always been in complete agreement with me about your men, both about their good points and—shall we say—their less fortunate ones? He has always retreated into himself about it, except for that one time when he got upset over Tom and telegraphed Bennington that you weren't coming back. I've been the one who has battled out in the open and taken the brunt of your defiance and hostility . . . Do see it this way: You are an absolutely terrific girl. Everyone who has

known you always has thought you were destined for a brilliant future. Almost every man who meets you finds you unusually desirable; almost every mother would like to have you for a daughter-in-law. Of how many of the men you've gone for can you say this is true, in corresponding terms? How could we help being concerned? How can we not care what kind of man you marry?

5) We shall try our best to be "civilized" and "sophisticated" about your affairs from now on. But we do beg you to be discreet and dignified. It's an old cliché, almost a piece of folk wisdom, that the "smartest" girls are the ones no one can ever "prove" anything about. As for Lewis, I hope he and Daddy can get to know each other better and reach some sort of acceptance. I don't dislike him, in fact, I'm really "fond" of him and respect his "mind." And I'm glad for your sake that he's a writer—I think writing is one of the activities that really count, if it's authentic. And I'm sure his is. About marriage: Frankly, if he were my son and I cared about his continuing to grow as a writer, I'd not want to see him take on the burdens of marriage so young, before he's established. It's too precarious, too dependent on a lot of complex factors, too precious to hazard. And I care about your career, too, and would like to see you really concentrate on developing your skills and establish yourself as a person in your own right before tying yourself down. You're just finally getting free of dependency on us: why give up your freedom? Up to now you've always had Bennington as an escape, and your jobs were always self-limiting; don't take on too many responsibilities at once. I still feel that you have many things—good ones—within yourself that you aren't aware of and must try out to be fully your best

self, and it will take time. So don't *rush* into anything that would limit you. Marriage is a complete other world from an affair.

6)   I'm sorry you mind my being "insulting," but I prefer cynicism to sentimentality. Would you rather I talked like Mrs. Norman Vincent Peale? (See enclosure.) As for "Angel Hair," I've tried to explain to you what that was all about and it's a perfectly real reaction.

7)   I'm not really sorry I upset you because I am sure you can "take" it a lot better than I've taken my own "hurts." I *have* to be honest with you. I do want you to be honest with me, but, more importantly, I want you to be honest with yourself. The turning-point in my life, when everything fell into place, was when I learned what the word "rationalization" means. Since then I've never been fooled by myself or by anyone else. I know sometimes it's a good and therapeutic process, but I'm glad I can do without it and I hope you'll eventually be able to.

8)   I was exactly like you in feeling I had to be "in love" in order to do my best work, but my own experience taught me that this is a supreme feminine fallacy. Perhaps your experience will teach you differently, but beware—keep a little reserve of doubt. *I* think being in love dulls the wits. Men don't feel this way, not if they are truly creative. They keep love in its place and put their art first—and they may do without love for a season but they can't leave their art alone. I am sure this is why the greatest things to date have been done by men. Love is fine, and all that, but don't let it be a trap for your gifts.

Leo saw the doctor: Joanie's trouble is that she's still emotionally hung up over Curtis, though she gave him up long ago in her mind. (I learned what the trouble was there, will tell you sometime, it's sort of strange.) The doctor advised L. to hang around for a while as a "supporting presence" though not necessarily nearby, so she'll leave for the Cape Wed. to stay with the Chavchavadzes for a time and keep in touch. So you may see her at some point.

                              Much, much love, darling baby,
                              Mummy

Wednesday

P.S.

Just to reiterate, so you'll have no doubt about it, that you need not fear my "worry" and "emotionalism." Daddy came home for lunch and got your letter, so I know what you've decided. Well, good luck in your work. I hope you'll always be open-minded and willing to learn, and never be afraid to admit you could do better. And don't be afraid to ask me for advice or suggestions if you can take them impersonally; I'm much more objective about you than you've ever realized. The tears have been unfortunate, I know, but you must understand they are my way of handling the strain of knowing too much and wanting too much. People never really can avoid conflict and I prefer to face it rather than kid myself. I see you and Daddy still believe the fiction that I'm a "problem." You're perfectly welcome to it if it comforts you. But things are not always what they seem. No matter, I'm sure it's a useful fiction to him, and my job now that you are taken care of is to make sure he keeps his balance. Actually, though, he's the one who's really emotional beyond reason. You'll always be welcome and accepted and there's no reason why seeing each other can't be fun. I'm awfully glad you decided against a complete break, because that wouldn't have been fun. Some cooperation from you will be necessary in this arrangement—perhaps I'll have to pretend you're living with another Bennington girl or something, if we have many visitors. But that shouldn't present difficulties if we agree and keep it straight. I want to feel free with you myself, but I've certainly no intention of trying to run your life now that you've made your final choice. I'll continue to hope that you grow in wisdom and that you have good fortune, but I'll keep my feelings to myself. It seems to me that most of my life has been spent watching people become less than they could have been because of some little piece of trivial bad luck, or unwillingness to get perspective on themselves, or failure to make a "leap" forward because it would be too much work or too painful, but I've always felt that you were going to be the exception and bring me great pride and pleasure.

This is *really* the curtain for my role as your mother, unless you should ever need or want a little "mothering" care yourself. I don't even want to be called "Mummy" anymore and certainly not "Mother," so I guess you'll just have to call me Frances. Love, etc.

Wednesday, 1 June 1966

Dearest Annie,

Bill Berkson asked me last night to congratulate you on ANGEL HAIR, and said he hoped you'd be coming to his classes sometime. Peter Schjeldahl thanked me for sending it to him and said it's a "beautiful magazine." Also, yesterday morning Holland came over and I showed it to her over our coffee klatsch. She read your poem and seemed amazed, then read it again, and she said, "I never knew Anne could write like that, she must have been working very hard, it's a fine poem and very moving."

Well, this session of poetry is over and it's definitely been worth it for me every minute. Apart from enjoying the pure exercise of intelligence I've learned more about how to "place" poetry with some supporting background for my own judgments, which previously were almost totally instinctual, though happily I found out that I was never too far off the "mark." It's introduced me to a lot of areas of Literature I'd never paid much attention to, the French poets, the surrealists, Joyce—though that wasn't really introduction but a stimulus. And it's been lively fun. The effects on my own writing have been all good, too; I've gotten away from a lot that was unnecessary and extraneous, and gotten glimpses of many interesting possibilities for myself. BB said he likes my "new" things very much. He read one of them for discussion last night, "Dependency." The discussion for the whole evening was general, more or less taking the opportunity to touch on, or ask about, anything anyone might feel hadn't yet been covered. Bernadette Mayer had done a sestina called "The Aeschyleans" which he also read; it's very Greek in all its conceptions, her images and concepts are almost completely true to some of *my* opinions about ancient Greece (*turbulent stone* was one of the best.) It's going to be published in Ted Berrigan's "C Magazine." I think Schjeldahl's in love with her. (Lewis also asked me about that on account of his dedication of a poem to her in the newest "Mother.") He got very defensive about her poem when anyone criticised even a small thing about it: BB for instance thought some of the lines too slow; and I objected to a phrase, *sainted warriors* and to her use of the word "grace" in a Christian sense. But she told me after class that she thought I was right, and added that her whole idea had come from reading Nietzsche's *Birth of Tragedy*. A nice girl. She never opens her mouth in class, though; probably an introvert.

BB spoke of a lot of similarities between Ashbery and Auden, "somewhat similar life circumstances, not much in their poetry of the *self*—as in *self*-indulgence . . . their art is static, even dead, in the sense that it has reached its height, is finished, perfect." I gather *he* prefers this category of poetry himself. He likes Ginsberg, but finds that some of his things are spoiled (for him) by G's obsessions with his own experiences, emotions, his own person . . . Ashbery and Auden are more "civilized" in both a pejorative and a complimentary sense . . .Some discussion of Whitman, whose rolling, rhetorical, rhythmical poetic "speech" was the first and perhaps "only" American contribution to the poetic art . . . obvious influence on Williams, who used it with restraint, and on Ginsberg, who I guess uses it without restraint! BB wound up by saying there seem to be two kinds of people who really *enjoy* poetry: those who find emotional indulgence in it and it *reinforces* their own emotions ("it's so true!") . . . For the other sort it is entertainment (in the best sense of taking you *into* itself) of an *impersonal* nature, like religious contemplation of objects, so that what you are left with is not your own emotions, not the feeling of "commiserating" with others or having them "commiserate" with you. He didn't say what you *are* left with, but it seems clear enough that the difference is like that between, say, classicism and romanticism in general, though that isn't quite right because they overlap, and classicism has the connotation of "rigidity" and that's not what he meant. *You* think about it . . . As a final thought for the week he threw out, "To say that one can't take what seems to be cerebral in poetry may mean that one can't take the higher intellectual pursuits." . . . A gentlemanly way of saying those people are just not bright enough. He also talked about masturbation, interesting.

Carl arrived late last night, after I'd gotten home, with Phil Sayres (the boy from Villanova you met at Christmas, briefly) and Julian Zuckerman, (E.I. boy from upper Village) in Julian's car. They are going to be his roommates next year. I think Carl looks great. They're asleep now; Phil's going on to Philadelphia this afternoon.

Leo left for the Cape a little while ago. I shall miss her. She'll perhaps come by here in several weeks, depending on what Joanie can manage to work out for herself. The problem is tough, and in a way reminds me of what you went through over Nicky, except that your direction is outward when in difficulties and Joanie's is inward because of her terrible shyness. Her hysterical loudness, as you must have guessed, is just the obverse of that. And J's so disorganized in relation to every practical thing, still retreats into little-girlishness over housekeeping, bills, people, etc.

Daddy returned from Millville yesterday, in quite good spirits. He went straight to work in the morning so I didn't see him till dinnertime and then went out myself, but he told me about driving around the "new" lake with Lou and Dona and how completely different (and how ghastly) it is. The only, absolutely the *only* evidence left—momentarily, too—that we ever lived there is Carl's basketball backboard on a tree that's one of the few still standing. All the roads are designed for lots of traffic, all the houses are tasteless. But instead of getting him down I think seeing the place freed him from his obsession; he realized that paradise is really lost for him and he'll have to be more accepting of what he does have. In his own way he's already expressed this.

Much love to you, sweetie,
Mummy

Frances LeFevre: Poems 1963-1977

THE RECOGNITION

How can you tell when it will come?
Nothing has been scheduled for sure,
nothing is ever scheduled.
You open the door and it's there, that's all.

Perhaps a birdcall pierces through
the clear still air,
a twig snaps and falls,
or hoofbeats tap the hill.
These are signals
you may have heard before.
Now they are new.

You will have to be listening,
for you are the only one who can hear.
If you miss the sound at first
listen again, till you catch it.

And the shape, the shape you watch for,
is it strange, familiar, dim, bright?
You will not care.
All you will see is the face
behind the face,
the eyes looking out through the eyes
to the eyes behind your eyes.
All you will know is the shock of light
in the secret place.

                                          11 March 1963

WINSLOW

The blue donkey bead from Greece
we hung on his collar
looked charming against his white wire hair
but didn't ward off devils
the way it was supposed to.
For they certainly entered into him,
unless he was born with them,
Maybe he was, maybe dogs too
have an original taint like men,
though among the faithful only a heretic
would dare suggest it.

Anyway, there were devils in him,
in spite of his wagging tail. His black eyes
knew too much, his teeth were too eager
to nip the innocent limbs of little children
on the block. Finally he began biting me,
and I knew the blue bead was no talisman here
on Macdougal Street, and he had to go.

Does magic die when it's transplanted?
Would the bead have kept him out of trouble, say,
in a Greek village, would he have been placid
as a donkey in the sun, everybody's friend?
Years ago I had a dog there, a black and tan
shepherd, who hated ragged people.
Each morning when the milk woman with her jug
left the hills a mile away, he saw her coming
and set up such an uproar, so intent
on tearing her to pieces, that we gave up at last
and took our breakfast coffee black. We never thought
to put a donkey bead on him.

Once, on a road out of Jerusalem, all the dogs were barking.

13 March 1963

AFTER ATTENDING A VERY
PROPER CEREMONY

Greek Dora, friend of three of my friends,
threw away her wedding-dress because she did not like it
and put on her nightgown with a sash
and came down the stairs to meet her bridegroom
and married him.
They say the marriage was very happy.

Daughter, daughter, shall I go
to Klein's or Ohrbach's where the bargains are
and buy you an amusing nightgown
made in Italy, perhaps, with flame-colored designs?
Your grandmother's rosepoint lace
I've been saving for you so long
lies yellowing in the box,
which no one seems to want to open.

Or would you rather wear your old blue work shirt
and dungarees and sneakers?
I assure you it will be all right with me,
anything will.

'63

RETORT

"So nice to see you again,"
says the sign
on the pane
of the door
at the dime
store.

So sorry to state
that I honestly
cannot
reciprocate

17 August

PHILADELPHIA

Shall the cultural project workers take a bus,
a ferry, or the bridge train?
The sharp smell of soup burns above the river.
That's where they make it over there.
Nobody rides to hounds on that side.

The father-son-and-holy-ghost houses,
three rooms piled on one another,
occasionally house a prodigy,
which is great! Just knowing about it keeps
the tax-deductible checks coming.

But it's hard to make the parents see
why the kids should study Shakespeare
or act out Euripides in the hot summer street
while the gentlemen of the board are so
far away in Nantucket, St. Thomas, or Madrid.

THE UNDESIGNATED

Why not? We've already said goodbye
on the overhead bridge.
The council chamber's filling up fast
and soon the sky will resemble
the silvered wood of railroad ties
where ragwood grows too thickly in July.
That's all. Now, a bag of worms.
A hundred of us can't run down anything
except the clock with talk
and which way the wind.

"The target population will have to be included."
In the former coffin factory, now a school
the ceilings ooze tar and the windows let in
feathers. The beneficiaries of this learning
are traumatized, nailed down in the native
quarter. Coffee and sulphur fumes
are adulterated with perfumes.
The reading of the agenda
combines with obscenities
from the truck-loading platform.
It's a formative year.

At the outermost limits of the personal
a knocking in the pipes coincides
with the delivery of a telegram
which no one opens
because it will say yes or no
and force us to decide.

Workshop Assignment in O'Hara's Style

A LITTLE GREEK SUN

What is the matter with everybody
they have switched from instant coffee to instant tea
instant tea I'm so disappointed
yes didn't you know I detest it
it reminds me of somebody's old pipe tobacco
mixed with goat turds

come on let's get out of here
let's go to ZONAR'S for an ouzo
we can sit and watch the retired teachers from Iowa go by
hanging onto their pocketbooks
and the International Student Brigade go by
hanging onto their hair
maybe Melina Mercouri will come
and stop at our table and say "Hello, Yes"
like she did in Phaedra where she answered the phone
two octaves below middle C
if you ask me it was the only good thing in it
I really would rather Irene Pappas came by
in her latest haircut

it's only 10:30
and the light's so bright already
I think I'll have a pink ice-cream soda
what do you mean pink's the wrong color for 10:30 in the morning
would you rather I ordered pea-soup

wouldn't it be wonderful
if all these people went and cashed in all their Travelers Checks
at the same time and flooded the currency exchange with them

and caused a drachma and a national crisis
the king would ask the Prime Minister to form a new government
or resign
we wouldn't be able to get any more drachmas for ourselves
we'd be stranded on the island
and have to beg for our food—how romantic!
I've always thought I'd make a very appealing beggar
and as for you you'd be un succès fou
with your big brown eyes
yes you would in fact from now on I fully expect you
to support both of us with your begging
and I'll lie in a hammock and read Erotókritos
all day long in the sun

THE MARINERS

Wasn't it time? The landfall presumably made
Somewhat earlier than was unwittingly arranged for
Which was never the whole truth but only half
According to supposition and later proved correct
By dead reckoning. You have their skill to thank
For the course they taught you to steer
Beneath the Southern Cross, both there and not at all.
For in your precise belief you wanted to turn back
Or go forward altogether but the horizon stopped you.
The way the shadows of the crosstrees fell struck you
As significant and still provides a mood to retreat to
And hide in till the wind changes and you can watch
The dancing whitecaps. You are in love with the sea
All over again and the mast has become a tree of life.
Why shouldn't you climb it and touch the sky?
A young giant, you have not dreamed your strength.
Your friends appear content in every wind and weather
And will offer no argument. "Weather" is a word for
Non-fixation which presupposes adjustment or not caring
Too much since they can look elsewhere for entertainment.
From the mast the unreality of distance makes you wish
For home. As fantasies of reserve will conspire
To trap us in mists of inventiveness, so you now
Engage in navigation in which everything must be
Utterly honest if you are to avoid the shoals. You
Have still not been advised about the deviation or
Told frankly which sighting brings us closer to the
Morning star, because the charts are water-logged and the
Crew's memory unsure. But the captain himself will take
The soundings and he has promised to accept the final version

Of all that could be done but will probably collapse
In a failure of representation as soon as the
Pilot meets you at the channel's mouth and you
Are all in port by evening.

LEAVES

Perhaps the error was in the epilogue.
After accepting the malice of circumstance so
Openly we ought to have made an about-face
And sponsored hope, instead of treating it
As a leaven that would sour the bread.
In the unspent fortune, come to think of it
Were translucent and residual rhymes
Though no crossing light signalled "here is pardon"
Or "desist." The galaxy has a sound of chimes!
For, improvisation aside, I have learned
To love you within this semblance, where love
Is pejorative but doubly precious held in fee
And prepares a shade against the afterglow.

Quantities of sequins perforate the air
Giving a sense of sudden eloquence
As the keening swells and then subsides
Among the larches. Boys play soccer
In the court as if it were Elysium.
Distractions hang on the goal-posts
Like garlands. Odd, that one! Oh, well-done!
Lowering clouds are full of portents
And I wonder if I am losing my perspective.

I will try harder to erase what you deny.
This symbiosis gathers momentum.
I am almost persuaded that it is a matter
Of getting off the subway at a wrong station
Quite without intention but in time
To see the leaves turn.
How much does a superlative weigh, would you say?
I am giving you the benefit, a child's Christmas.

SHADOWS

Rivers go off the map
when they come to the sea.
So you, disconsolate that
flesh and memory are
perishable, ask to be
imaged by something more firm
than cloud-shapes. I agree.
This is hunger, not vanity.
I'd like to paint you on a
squinch in some small hillside
chapel by the Aegean, like a
saint, or carve you in green
steatite and keep you on my
mantel, to be looked at on
birthdays, or construct you out
of wire and mesh and glass.
I'd not aim at likeness,
just make sure the shadows
fell correctly. Shadows
are evidence that space
is filled, or light has
passed through. I shall
use them to show <u>you</u>.

CLEAR SKIES IN CENTRAL PARK

The year's ending for the lower school.
Teachers have extra work to do.
A day off! "Let's go to the park!"
Back to nature: trees and rocks are <u>real</u>.
Take sandwiches, make it a picnic.

They've seen the seals, bought the balloons,
done the merry-go-round three times.
Where can they eat and play while Mother rests?
Here's a grassy place with no people,
quiet and safe for two innocents.

No bench, so she sits cross-legged
on the ground. Skirt's a bit tight
but here who cares about knees and thighs?
She sees her children make discoveries:
sticks and stones, a beetle, ants and flies.

And now what's coming, a horse? It's stopping!
The mounted cop is talking.
"Don't think you better sit there, lady. Excuse me."
"Why not? Where's the NO TRESPASS sign? We <u>like</u> the grass."
He's young, he blushes deeply.

"Lady, there's a kind of creep across the way
with binoculars…"
"What? Oh. Well. I see. Thank you."
He blushes again, salutes, the horse trots on.
"Mummy. <u>What</u> did he say?"

17/2/77

Anghelos Sikelianos (1884-1951)
translated from the Greek by Frances LeFevre

THE SUICIDE OF ATZESIVANO
A DISCIPLE OF BUDDHA

Atzesivano took the knife
To himself impeccably. And his soul
At the instant he ended his life
Was a white dove. As a star will roll
Into the night from the farthest skies
Or an apple-blossom fall
At the touch of a gentle breeze
So the breath flew from his breast.

Such deaths are not a waste.
Only those who love life in its deepest
Essence may themselves reap the harvest
Of their existence, a single tall
Stalk of grain that calmly bends at last.

1977

Afterword

These letters were written to me by my mother during a few spirited and extremely substantive months in 1966. They are potent even now, stirring memories and associations, not least of which are early forays into a serious mind of poetry, apart and together. Frances LeFevre had an insatiable curiosity, which included poetry and the writing of it. I am ever in her debt for her refreshed sense of life lived inside this practice and study as well as the pleasures of urban artistic Kulchur. A way of life. On sitting behind Elliott Carter at a concert in New York City she is "as thrilled as a schoolgirl about a movie star."

The focus and anchor here is the Bill Berkson class. I was in my final spring semester at Bennington College while Frances was excited about studying with Bill, her first workshop with him. I had asked her to report on the doings.

I had travelled to Berkeley, California, the previous summer, encouraged by my friend from high school, Jonathan Cott, who was studying at UC Berkeley and was keeping me informed of political and cultural events on the west coast. At his urging my brother Carl and I caught a ride with a college mate and, after stopping to visit my mother's first husband Glafkos Sikelianos in Ojai, I went off alone to attend the Berkeley Poetry Conference. I subsequently met many of the participants at the readings and at adjacent after-hours events: Allen Ginsberg, Robert Duncan, Ted Berrigan, Ed Sanders, Ed Dorn, Lenore Kandel. I witnessed Charles Olson "enacting" his dismembering psyche from the stage and was inspired to a "vow to poetry" and "wild mind" poetics. I also met Lewis Warsh, young poet and novelist from New York City, and we bonded as cohorts and friends and founded Angel Hair Magazine and Books. Frank O'Hara couldn't be in Berkeley, although he was invited, nor could John Ashbery who was living in Paris. Ted Berrigan, holding up the New York School banner, read from his collaged sonnets, which in turn inspired Robert Duncan to write a series of sonnets in honor of Ted Berrigan's sonnets, and which we published first in *Angel Hair*. Lewis and I missed Allen Ginsberg's reading because we had taken LSD in San Francisco and couldn't get over the bridge. It was a heady and propitious time.

Meanwhile, Frances was already becoming steeped in contemporary poetry, abetted by my interest and growing commitment. Our burgeoning devotion found common ground. Her manic detailed epistles cover a range of material and experiments from Bill's class, in addition to a rhizomic shared world of family, friends, cultural figures, and beyond.

Raised in Yorktown PA, by a widowed mother who had converted to Christian Science, Frances dropped out of Vassar College, and went to Provincetown to pursue an interest in painting, met and married young, age 19, son of the celebrated poet Anghelos Sikelianos. She and Glafkos quickly boarded a ship to Greece and found themselves in the bosom of the Delphic Ideal, a community instituted by Glafkos's parents. She participated in the preparations for the staging of the second Delphic Festival under the auspices of her mother-in-law the entrepreneurial Eva Palmer Sikelianos, artist, weaver, directrice, an artistic curatorial "force" who was a mentor to my mother. Frances had a child with Glafkos, my brother Mark. There is reference in the letters to some of that history and people we knew mutually from the "Greek connection," but a new Ideal was taking over her sense of study and purpose, centered on the downtown New York poetry scene. She had married John Waldman, an itinerant musician at the time (they met at an Isamu Noguchi party) who went off to fight Nazis in Germany before I was born, and later studied at New York University and Columbia (earning a PhD) on the GI Bill, and landing a job at Pace University. He worked his way up to Secretary of the University. Frances and John had settled on Macdougal Street before I was born.

During the war Frances had worked for Con Edison, and was adept at providing an extra phone line at the house, free of charge. She also worked painting ties at a tie factory. Frances was busy during my childhood years, creative with her own projects, and following the various iterations of culture in New York. My parents were frugal, like many who had lived through the Depression. We were often "strapped" financially, a word she often used when I was a child, which I came to loathe for its images of bondage and restriction. But as John's position at Pace improved, they could afford tickets to cultural events like the Metropolitan Opera. As the first members of their families to go to college, they were committed to making sure my brother and I had the same opportunity.

She had her translation projects with Sikelianos's poetry, her own ongoing reading and writing practices, including the more focused poems that were encouraged by the workshops with Bill Berkson.

I couldn't keep up with Frances half the time. She had a charged almost aspirational energy, to *know* and to understand what made people tick; to know more about poetry, about how *that* worked, to also further trust and develop her intellect. She would be awake late at night my high school years waiting for me to come home, urging friends escorting me to the door to enter and to continue our conversation with *her* included.

My mother had an ever-widening circle of friends from other worlds as well, as evidenced in these letters to me. She was close to creative people, loved the exchange of ideas, of affections. Was hungry for them. Her letters were demanding, she wanted my attention, had it, but my own responses were often cursory and too few. She also wanted me to make something of myself artistically. She once said that if she found me too early pushing a baby carriage down the street she'd "haul off and kill me." I used to joke with friends about my mother behaving like a jealous lover. It's of course relevant in her concern for me that Frances had felt stymied by two marriages and children. Granted, she was in a unique situation in Greece, but by 1945 she was having a new family under "straighter" post-war USA circumstances. She suffered I know, in feeling she had not realized her own potential as an artist.

The fierce letter to me as I am about to leave college (May 29, 1966) was—in retrospect—quite risky to our friendship. She was upset about my love life, saying that "being in love dulls the wits," "is a supreme feminine fallacy" and that men never let love get in the way of their art. "This is really the curtain for my role as your mother." I was upset but also annoyed at her conservatism. She cared what people thought . . . to be a "slut" was anathema, horror of horrors. Her own first marriage was not happy at the end, there had been affairs, abortions, a French suitor. (I recently realized I might have inherited a ring given him from her.) I certainly didn't consider myself promiscuous (a pejorative, simplistic word that never adequately describes sexual adventure); had confidence in the things I was interested in—theatre and poetry. I saw the relationship with Lewis as a generative one and Angel Hair as a serious project. And marriage would be part of our landscape as artists. But how could she know this? Our decision to live together and subsequent marriage was initially hard on her, although she came to appreciate our early spirited partnership in poetry. Later, she would understand that Lewis and I were allies in helping build a flourishing poetry community. She clearly took pride in the first issue of *Angel Hair*, checking how sales were faring at the 8th Street Bookshop.

In retrospect, an extraordinary irony underlies some of this early history. One can't predict how the life stream of particular beings in "consociational" time, a term borrowed from anthropologist Clifford Geertz referring to the generational and social interconnect of beings, will unfold. What relationships, intimacies will develop and morph, how friendship will survive. How creative work will be generated, how collaborations and friendships will continue for decades, as they have in my life. And what creativity and life-altering shifts will follow from these junctures. Frank O'Hara and Allen Ginsberg were already heroes to me and I emulated their examples as "centers" of artistic and cultural activity and their own radical poetry, but this was at a time early in my formation as a poet. They ultimately gave a permission of imagination to others with their generosity and friendship. I already felt this in Berkeley with Allen when I first met him. I met Frank officially, only once, before his tragic death, when he told me to come and be a volunteer at MoMA. I saw Bill as a "lineage holder" to Frank and to John Ashbery and Kenneth Koch.

Frances died in 1982, age 71, of complications of diabetes. This was a huge loss. Unfathomable. Frances has been a muse and friend in inestimable ways. I sometimes think I have spent my whole life working to please her. Certainly the conversation continues with her in my head. Before she died she had been acting the part of "the spirit of heroin" in a theatrical production of William Burroughs's *Naked Lunch*. By then she had even more decisively crossed over to the avant-garde. And I was caught up with the nurturing of the Jack Kerouac School of Disembodied Poetics at Naropa in Boulder and in a new relationship.

That didn't mean that the old friendships/relationships would end, rather they might shift. Some would see this web of attractions and affiliations as nothing short of incestuous! It's certainly an unusual and fascinating history. Bill Berkson became a close friend who moved downtown, around the corner from the apartment Lewis and I shared at 33 St Mark's Place, where I settled after graduating from Bennington and started working at The Poetry Project at St. Mark's Church-In-the-Bowery, the center for much of our activity. Lewis and I were married in 1967, and after separating amicably, I lived with Michael Brownstein some years. Bernadette Mayer became a close and intimate friend as well and later married Lewis and started a family. I founded the Jack Kerouac School with Allen Ginsberg and Diane di Prima in Boulder in 1974, and had a parallel life in Boulder for many years with Reed Bye, and raising our son Ambrose together. My brother Carl was a caretaker of Allen Ginsberg's farm in Cherry Valley in the early '70s after graduating from college, which led to his settling and raising his own family in that upstate haven.

Filmmaker Ed Bowes, who was living with Bernadette in 1966, and I were married in 2002. Angel Hair Magazine and Books published work and books by Bill Berkson, Bernadette Mayer, Peter Schjeldahl, and Hannah Weiner over the years. Lewis's United Artists Books published Bernadette Mayer's *Utopia* in which Bernadette dedicates a section of the book "to Frances LeFevre." Lewis Warsh and I also edited *The Angel Hair Anthology* (2002) in which all these poets appear. I stopped in Santa Barbara on that first trip out west heading to Berkeley, I held the newborn Eleni Sikelianos, daughter of my "step-brother" Jon. Eleni later graduated from The Jack Kerouac School, and is herself a prodigious poet.

Under the imprint Erudite Fangs I published *The Border Guards*, Frances's translation from the Greek of Anghelos Sikelianos. Frances also published a book of Surrealist César Moro's poems *Amour à Mort* translated from the French, a language in which she was quite proficient, with the elegant Rotating Triangle Press. She also had a stint as an editor of the Poetry Project Newsletter. I remember getting a postcard from Ted Berrigan, amused by seeing my parents at St. Mark's Church Poetry Project "licking the stamps."

In re-reading these letters after many years I am struck by Frances's dislike of aspects of Allen Ginsberg's poetry, a not uncommon visceral reaction for some. Later she would proclaim that Allen and John Ashbery—although worlds apart—were her two favorite poets. I always loved a line of one of Frances's poems: "Quantities of sequins perforate the air/Giving a sense of sudden eloquence." They seem to radiate her shimmering aspiration for a poetry that is not expensive or pretentious, yet stays challenging, and her deep passion and love of eloquence.

—Anne Waldman, 2015

Glossary of Names

NOTE: This listing includes friends and acquaintances of Frances LeFevre and Anne Waldman. It is by no means a complete who's who of these letters. Some people remain a mystery, as they do in life. We generally chose not to include writers studied and discussed in the letters, unless those writers also show up in Frances's daily life. People are listed in order of appearance.

Frances LeFevre Waldman: In addition to writing her own poetry, Frances LeFevre translated from Greek and French. Her translation of César Moro's *Amour à Mort* was published by Leandro Katz and Ted Castle's Vanishing Rotating Triangle Press. An excerpt was recently selected by Cecilia Vicuña for inclusion in *The Oxford Book of Latin American Poetry*. Her translation of *The Border Guards*, by Angelos Sikelianos, was published by Anne Waldman's Erudite Fangs Press. She was Editor of the Poetry Project Newsletter in 1977 and often helped out at collating parties for Poetry Project publications.

Frances met her first husband, Glafkos Sikelianos, in the United States in 1929. They almost immediately married and set sail for Greece. Frances quickly got involved with preparations for the second Delphic Festival, organized by her parents-in-law, Eva Palmer Sikelianos and poet Angelos Sikelianos. Frances spoke of her time in Greece as the highlight of her life, and remained fascinated by the culture and poetry long after her return to the States in 1939.

She met her second husband, John Waldman, shortly after her return to the States. She had one child with Glafkos, Mark Sikelianos, and two with John, Anne and Carl Waldman.

Anne Waldman: Anne Waldman helped create the "Outrider" experimental poetry community, a culture she has nurtured for over four decades as writer, editor, teacher, performer, magpie scholar, infra-structure curator, and cultural/political activist. Her poetry is recognized in the lineage of Whitman and Ginsberg, and in the Beat, New York School, and Black Mountain trajectories of the New American Poetry. She is the author of more than forty books, including *Fast Speaking Woman, Vow to Poetry,* and several selected poems editions including *Helping the Dreamer, Kill or Cure,* and *In the Room of Never Grieve*. She has concentrated on the long poem as a cultural intervention with such projects as *Marriage: A Sentence, Structure of The World Compared to a Bubble, Manatee/Humanity, Gossamurmur,* and the anti-war feminist epic *The Iovis Trilogy: Colors in the Mechanism of Concealment,* a twenty-five-year project.

She was one of the founders and directors of The Poetry Project at St. Mark's Church In-the-Bowery, working there for twelve years. In 1974, she co-founded with Allen Ginsberg the Jack Kerouac School of Disembodied Poetics at Naropa University. She is a Distinguished Professor of Poetics at Naropa and continues to work to preserve the school's substantial literary/ oral archive.

She has collaborated extensively with a number of artists, musicians, and dancers, including George Schneeman, Elizabeth Murray, Richard Tuttle, Donna Dennis, and Pat Steir, and the theatre director Judith Malina. She has also been working most recently with other media including audio, film and video, with her husband, writer and video/film director Ed Bowes, and with her son, musician and composer Ambrose Bye. *Publishers Weekly* recently referred to Waldman as "a counter-cultural giant." In 2015, she received the American Book Award for Lifetime Achievement from the Before Columbus Foundation.

Bill Berkson: Bill Berkson is a poet, critic, teacher and sometime curator. He is the author of some thirty books and pamphlets of poetry, including *Gloria*, a portfolio of poems with etchings by Alex Katz; *Portrait and Dream: New & Selected Poems*; and *Expect Delays*. His collaborative works include *Hymns of St. Bridget & Other Writings* with Frank O'Hara; *What's Your Idea of a Good Time?: Letters & Interviews 1977-1985* with Bernadette Mayer; *BILL* with drawings by Colter Jacobsen; *Ted Berrigan* with George Schneeman; *Not an Exit* with Léonie Guyer; and *Repeat After Me* with John Zurier.

During the 1960s he was an editorial associate at *Art News*, a regular contributor to *Arts*, guest editor at the Museum of Modern Art, associate producer of a public television program on art, and taught literature and writing workshops at the New School for Social Research and Yale University. After moving to Northern California in 1970, he began editing and publishing a series of poetry books and magazines under the Big Sky imprint. He also taught regularly in the California Poets in the Schools program.

In the mid-1980s he resumed writing art criticism on a regular basis, contributing monthly reviews and articles to *Artforum* and other magazines. He is a corresponding editor for *Art in America* and a contributing editor at *artcritical.com*. Recent collections of criticism include *The Sweet Singer of Modernism & Other Art Writings*, *Sudden Address: Selected Lectures 1981-2006,* and *For The Ordinary Artist*. *Parties du corps,* a selection of his poetry in French translation, was published in 2011. He is currently professor emeritus at the San Francisco Art Institute and divides his time between San Francisco and New York.

Peter Schjeldahl: Participant in Bill Berkson's poetry workshop. He is an art critic and poet. He has been a staff art critic for *The New Yorker* since 1998, and his art criticism has been featured in *ARTNews, The New York Times*, and *The Village Voice*. A collection of his New Yorker pieces was published in 2008 as *Let's See: Writings on Art from The New Yorker*. His first collection of poetry, *White Country*, was published by Corinth Books. Anne Waldman and Lewis Warsh published another collection, *Dreams*, under Angel Hair Books in 1973.

Bernadette Mayer: Participant in Bill Berkson's poetry workshop. Four of her early books were published by Angel Hair Books. With Vito Acconci, she edited the journal *0 to 9* from 1967-69. She also established United Artists Magazine and Books with then husband Lewis Warsh. She served as Director of The Poetry Project from 1980 to 1984. Works include *Midwinter Day, A Bernadette Mayer Reader, Memory, What's Your Idea of a Good Time?: Letters and Interviews 1977-1985* with Bill Berkson, *Ethics of Sleep*, and *The Helens of Troy, NY*.

Jean Cott: Mother of Jonathan Cott. Family friend of the Waldmans.

Carl Waldman: Son of Frances LeFevre and John Waldman. He is a writer, musician, and producer. His books include *Encyclopedia of Native American Tribes* and *Atlas of the North American Indian*. He worked as an archivist at the New York State Historical Society in Cooperstown, NY. He also served as the caretaker of Allen Ginsberg's house in Cherry Valley, home of the Committee on Poetry.

Jonathan Cott: Close high school friend of Anne Waldman's. He is a poet and critic, and contributing editor for *Rolling Stone Magazine*. He has published a number of important collections of *Rolling Stone* interviews, including *The Ballad of John and Yoko*, edited by Jacqueline Kennedy for Doubleday Books. His work was published in the first issue of *Angel Hair*.

Angelica Heinegg Clark: An actress from New Zealand, Angelica occasionally travelled to New York. She dated Jonathan Cott and in 1968 married Tom Clark at St Mark's Church In-The-Bowery.

Mr. & Mrs. Marianne Boelitz: Friends and neighbors of Frances's. Anne was good friends with their son, Martin, during high school, and remained close with the family, particularly Marianne.

Michael Brownstein: Participant in Bill Berkson's workshop. He is a poet and novelist. His books include *Self-Reliance* and *World on Fire*. His work addresses conscious transformation, combining poetry, personal narrative, and cultural commentary.

John Waldman: Frances's second husband, and father of Anne and Carl Waldman. John and Frances met in 1939 or 1940 at a party hosted by artist Isamu Noguchi. At the time, John was a swing piano player. He served in World War II, after which he studied at NYU and Columbia on the GI Bill. He became a professor of journalism and literature at Pace University. After retirement from Pace he volunteered at a methadone clinic helping clients with educational goals. He is the author of *Rapid Reading Made Simple*, as well as several other books.

Jean Boudin: Frances's best friend and neighbor. She was a poet and often attended readings and events with Frances. She was married to civil rights lawyer, Leonard Boudin. They had two children, Michael and Kathy. Michael also went into law, serving as a judge. Kathy Boudin was one of the co-founders of the radical activist organization Weather Underground. After over a decade in hiding, she served twenty-two years in prison for her role in an armed robbery and felony murder. While in prison she helped found a number of educational programs and wrote and published poetry.

Shirley Broughton: Friend of Frances's. Founder of NY's Theatre for Ideas. Co-producer of *Town Bloody Hall*, focused around an April 30, 1971 Town Hall event discussing Women's Liberation and featuring Germaine Greer, Diana Trilling, Jill Johnston, Jacqueline Ceballos and Norman Mailer. The Town Hall event was also organized by Broughton and the Theatre for Ideas.

Leonard Boudin: Civil liberties lawyer and activist. His landmark cases include representing Daniel Ellsberg in the release of the Pentagon Papers. He also represented a number of opponents to the Viet Nam war, and successfully argued that draft resisters could not be stripped of their citizenship without due process.

Helen Eisner: Friend of Frances's. Playwright. Writer of *Penny Change*, which played for one night on October 16, 1963 at Players Theatre on Macdougal Street.

Dorothy Rogers Grotz: Friend of Frances's. A painter best known for her post-impressionist style landscape work.

Paul Grotz: Husband of Dorothy Rogers Grotz. An architect, photographer, art director and managing editor of *Architectural Forum*. He co-founded the magazine *Architecture Plus*.

Paul Gray: Theatre and film director. He was the head of Bennington College's Drama Department during Anne Waldman's time there as a student.

Nina Travlos: Daughter of Iōannēs (John) and Elly Travlos. Iōannēs was a celebrated architectural archeologist who worked on the restoration of the Stoa of Attalos in Athens. Anne Waldman lived with their family in Greece in 1963. Nina married and settled in Brooklyn, New York.

Holland Taylor: Frances's upstairs neighbor. Holland was pursuing stage acting at the time, but had her breakthrough role in the sitcom *Bosom Buddies* in 1980. She won an Emmy for her role in *The Practice*, and is well known for her role in *Two and a Half Men*.

Tom Griffin: Friend of Anne's. They worked together at a Quaker arts center in Philadelphia over the summer of 1962, serving at risk children.

Marian Tracy: Friend of Frances's. Cookbook writer whose titles include *The Peasant Cookbook, Casserole Cookery Complete*, and *Cooking Under Pressure*.

Gay Harriman: College friend of Anne Waldman's.

Donald Gardiner: Poet and translator of Octavio Paz and Ernesto Cardenal. He founded a group of street poets, Guerilla Poets, in 1968 in London, where he also performed with the London group of the Living Theatre.

Simone Juda: College friend of Anne Waldman's. She lived with Frances at Macdougal Street during a Bennington non-resident term.

Angelos (Anghelos) Sikelianos: Renowned Greek poet, he was a candidate for the Nobel Prize in Literature in 1949. Father of Glafkos Sikelianos, Frances's first husband. In 1982, Frances published a translation of his work *The Border Guards, Poems of the Greek Resistance (1940-1946)*.

Cyril Peters: Director of Cultural Programming at WRVR. Anne Waldman worked with him curating and producing a poetry series for the station during her 1965 Bennington non-resident semester.

Marianne Moore: Poet associated with the Imagist and Modernist movement. Recipient of the National Book Award and Pulitzer Prize.

Hannah Weiner: Participant in Bill Berkson's workshop. She is often associated with the Language poets and was involved in early happenings in the 1960s in New York. An early manuscript, *The Clairvoyant Journal*, was published by Angel Hair. Later works include *We Speak Silent* and *Hannah Weiner's Open House*. Her work incorporates her experience with seeing words projected on people's foreheads and schizophrenia, particularly with how the illness affected her relationship to language.

Elsie Orahley: As a teenager, Elsie lived first with William Carlos Williams's family, then with Ann Harris's family. Williams's poem "To Elsie" is named for her.

Ann Harris: Family friends of Frances and John Waldman. They lived in Paterson, New Jersey.

Mark Sikelianos: Son of Glafkos Sikelianos and Frances LeFevre. He was born in Greece and returned to the States with Frances and Glafkos in 1939. He lived with Frances and John at Macdougal Street and went to New York's High School of Music and Art. He worked at Broadcast Music Incorporated (BMI) for many years.

Chuck Stein: Charles Stein is a poet, translator, and scholar of Charles Olson's work. *The Virgo Poem* was published by Angel Hair Books in 1967. Other books include *The Hat Rack Tree, From Mimir's Head*, and translations of *The Odyssey* and *The Iliad*.

Sam Shepard: Playwright, actor, and director. Recipient of the 1979 Pulitzer Prize for Drama for his play *Buried Child*. He was associated with Theatre Genesis at St. Mark's Church-in-the-Bowery. Anne Waldman produced his play, *Icarus*, for WRVR in 1965, as part of her poetry series during Bennington's non-resident semester. In 2009, he received the PEN/Laura Pels International Foundation for Theatre Award as a master American dramatist.

Marin Riley: Actress. At the time of the letters she was working on the TV series *Dark Shadows*.

Marshall McLuhan: Philosopher often cited as the father of communications and media theory. Author of *The Mechanical Bride, The Gutenberg Galaxy*, and *Understanding Media*, in which he coined the phrase "the medium is the message."

Jim Rooney: Anne Waldman met Rooney while he was in Greece on a Fulbright in 1963/4 and they traveled together for a short while. He is a musician, songwriter, and musical engineer and producer. His memoir, *In It for the Long Run: A Musical Odyssey*, was published in 2014. He has collaborated with Bill Monroe, Alison Krauss, Muddy Waters, and Nanci Griffith. He is based in Nashville.

Stephanie Gordon: A psychologist. At the time of these letters she was living with Kenneth Noland, they married the following year.

Kenneth Noland: American abstract painter, and one of the best known Color Field artists. His work is represented at major galleries and museums nationally and internationally. He studied at the renowned Black Mountain College.

Lewis Warsh: Anne Waldman's first husband, they met at the Berkeley Poetry Conference. Co-founder (with Anne) of Angel Hair Magazine and Books. Co-founder (with Bernadette Mayer) of United Artists Magazine and Books. He is the author of over twenty-five books of poetry and fiction and was the founding director of the MFA program in creative writing at Long Island University in Brooklyn. His most recent books include *Alien Abduction* and *One Foot Out the Door: Collected Stories*.

Marie Farnsworth: A pioneer in archeological science. Her primary focus was the study of Greek pottery. In 1980 she was awarded the inaugural Pomerance Award for Scientific Contributions to Archaeology by the Archaeological Institute of America.

Yeffe Kimball: Born Effie Y. Goodman, Kimball became known as an Osage artist. Her work was influenced by American Indian spiritual symbols and by the themes of her husband Harvey Slatin's work in atomic science. With Edna Massey, she collaborated on a documentary project producing more than 5,500 images of American Indians over a ten-year period. Since her death, her Osage heritage has been disputed.

Harvey Slatin: Atomic scientist who worked on the isolation of plutonium at the Manhattan Project in Los Alamos. J. Robert Oppenheimer was the faculty advisor for his doctoral thesis in nuclear physics. He later refused to work on weapons of war and turned his attention to electroplating processes. He was married to Yeffe Kimball at the time of these letters.

Robert David Cohen: Poet and journalist. He has worked as a journalist at the UN and speechwriter and communications officer at UNICEF. He co-edited *El Corno Emplumado/The Plumed Horn* with Margaret Randall in Mexico in 1968-9. He worked with Anne Waldman at the Poetry Project in 1966.

David Grimm: Actor and close friend of Anne Waldman's. They met at Stratford, CT, where they were both working for the Stratford Shakespeare Festival.

Lee Roberts: Frances's next door neighbor.

Ted Wilentz: Brothers Ted and Eli Wilentz owned the Eighth Street Bookshop. As the founder of Corinth Books, he published works by Jack Kerouac, Diane di Prima and Allen Ginsberg. Corinth Books published Anne Waldman's first book, *Giant Night*.

Andrea Dworkin: Feminist, author, and anti-pornography activist. Works include *Pornography: Men Possessing Women, Intercourse,* and her autobiography *Heartbreak: The Political Memoir of a Feminist Militant.* She attended Bennington College with Anne Waldman. In 1965, while a student at Bennington, she was arrested during a protest against the war in Viet Nam. Her grand jury testimony about a brutal internal examination during her detention made international news. She and Anne stayed in contact, and Anne talked her out of a planned boycott of a William S. Burroughs reading at The Poetry Project in 1973.

John Perreault: Poet, art curator, and art critic. From 1964-1966, he published the mimeo magazine *Elephant.* The magazine included work by Anne Waldman, Lewis Warsh, Ted Berrigan, and many others in the New York School circle. He wrote for *ArtNews, the Village Voice*, and *Soho News*, and blogged at artopia at artjournal.com.

David Amram: Composer and musician often associated with the Beats. He was a close collaborator of Jack Kerouac, which he wrote about in *Offbeat: Collaborating with Kerouac,* and composed the music for Robert Frank and Alfred Leslie's film *Pull My Daisy.* He has been a guest at Naropa University, including visits during the 1982 Kerouac Conference and 2007 Kerouac Festival. In 1966, the year of these letters, he was selected as the New York Philharmonic's first composer-in-residence. In 2011, he was inducted into the Oklahoma Jazz Hall of Fame and given their Jay McShann Lifetime Achievement Award. David and Anne Waldman dated in the 1960s.

Joseph Papp: Theatre producer and director. Founder of The Public Theater, a NY arts organization that established the New York Shakespeare Festival, or Shakespeare in the Park. After finding a permanent home for the festival in Central Park, Papp took over the former Astor Library in the East Village as the headquarters for The Public Theater in 1967. They opened with the world premiere of *Hair*.

Joanie Cook: Daughter of Leo and Harl Cook. Harl knew John Waldman and Glafkos Sikelianos from Provincetown and remained friendly with both of them. Joanie lived upstairs to the Waldmans and later dated Carl Waldman.

Kim Hunter: Actress best known for her Academy Award winning role as Stella Kowalski in *A Streetcar Named Desire*. Her daughter, Kathryn Emmett, was Anne Waldman's best friend in high school. They lived a few blocks away from the Waldmans in the Village. Anne Waldman lived with Kim and Kathryn during the 1961 Stratford Shakespeare Festival, where Kim performed and Anne worked backstage.

Glafkos (Glaukos) Sikelianos: Frances's first husband. They met in 1929 when he was visiting the US. They married and almost immediately moved to Greece. They arrived just in time for the second Delphic Festival, organized by Glafkos's parents, Angelos and Eva Sikelianos. They returned to the States in 1939, the year they divorced. They both went on to have other families, and their progeny stayed close.

Ted Berrigan: Poet often associated with the second generation New York School Poets. His book *The Sonnets* remains a staple of contemporary poetics. Close friend of Anne Waldman, with whom he collaborated on the long poem *Memorial Day*, composed for a 1971 Memorial Day reading at the Poetry Project. *The Collected Poems of Ted Berrigan*, edited by Alice Notley with Anselm Berrigan and Edmund Berrigan was published in 2005.

Nicky Munger: Village friend of Anne Waldman's.

★★★

The Editor

Lisa Birman is the author of *How To Walk Away* and *For That Return Passage—A Valentine for the United States of America*. With Anne Waldman, she co-edited the anthology *Civil Disobediences: Poetics and Politics in Action*. She has published several chapbooks of poetry, including *deportation poems*, and her work has appeared in *Revolver, Floor Journal, Milk Poetry Magazine, Trickhouse, Poetry Project Newsletter*, and *not enough night*. Lisa served as the Director of the Summer Writing Program at Naropa University's Jack Kerouac School of Disembodied Poetics for twelve years.

Acknowledgments

Bill Berkson; Judy Hussie-Taylor; Ron Padgett; Mac McGinnes; Kathleen Dow; The Anne Waldman Papers, University of Michigan Library (Special Collections Library); Ed Bowes; Max Regan; Kate Koepke; HR Hegnauer; Gina Sikelianos.

Frances LeFevre and Anne Waldman,
New York City, 1966. Photograph by
Lewis Warsh.